UNWRITTEN RULES FOR YOUR CAREER

"Helpful tips on leadership for employees at all levels and at all career stages."

David Campbell
Center for Creative Leadership

"Takes much of the mystery out of career success."

Robert J. House
The Wharton School, University of Pennsylvania

"I would have liked to have read this book very early in my career before I made so many mistakes. I would still have made my share of them, but certainly there would have been far fewer."

Milton J. Schloss
retired Chairman, Beatrice Foods

"In the best tradition of do-it-yourself career management."

Joseph A. Steger
President, University of Cincinnati
formerly of Colt Industries

"Graen has a keen eye for small things in large organizations that make a huge difference."

Karl Weick
former Editor, *Administrative Science Quarterly*

UNWRITTEN RULES FOR YOUR CAREER

The 15 Secrets for Fast-Track Success

GEORGE B. GRAEN

WILEY

JOHN WILEY & SONS
New York • Chichester • Brisbane • Toronto • Singapore

Library of Congress Cataloging in Publication Data:

Graen, George B.
    Unwritten rules for your career: the 15 secrets for fast-track success.
        p. cm.
    Bibliography: p.
    ISBN 0-471-61490-4
    1. Career development.   2. Organizational effectiveness.
I. Title.
HF5549.5.C35G73   1989
650.1′4—dc20   89-32007
                                                                      CIP

Printed in the United States of America

10 9 8 7 6 5 4 3 2 1

Preface

Why—and how—do some people in organizations seem to rise quickly through the ranks, receiving frequent promotions and generous salary increases, while others advance much more slowly and modestly in their careers? For more than 20 years my research partners and I have sought answers to this enigma. In doing so, we have systematically observed, tested, interviewed, surveyed, counseled, trained, evaluated, and analyzed thousands of people in hundreds of organizations in the United States and Japan. We have studied people at all levels of private and public, large and small, national and multinational organizations in a variety of industries. We have examined manufacturing organizations from aerospace and automotive to steel and textiles, and we have researched service organizations from accounting and banking to retail and utilities. Throughout our studies, we have consistently insisted on using whatever means necessary to obtain high-quality data. Equally important, we have required that each interpretation of our data be confirmed by the fast-trackers who've risen quickly to the top in many of these organizations.

Three key ideas surfaced from our studies:

1. The fast-trackers who earn frequent promotions and generous financial rewards have a clear understanding of the unwritten

rules that govern organizations, and they use that understanding to manage their careers.

2. Organizations are wise to reward these savvy fast-trackers because the fast-trackers strengthen and advance the interests of their companies as effectively as they do their own careers. In fact, organizations increasingly need as many fast-trackers as they can get.

3. Many potential fast-trackers and the organizations in which they work have suffered because the potential fast-trackers have not known these crucial unwritten rules.

My M.B.A. (Master's degree in Business Administration) students pointedly showed me the need to help potential fast-trackers avoid making career-threatening (and organization-jeopardizing) mistakes. Many eagerly encouraged me to share with a wider audience what I had learned about the unwritten rules of organizations. Some students were more adamant: They *demanded* to know why they weren't told about these unwritten rules before they disastrously damaged their careers by making what appeared to be naive blunders.

This book is for potential fast-trackers who, at whatever stage in their careers, seek to begin making valuable contributions to their companies and their careers by uncovering the unwritten rules of their organizations. If you did not learn about the unwritten rules from a family member or a friend and do not know its secrets, you are at a career disadvantage: You are struggling to balance on a unicycle while looking for the route to the fast track. This book will help you to trade your unwieldy unicycle for a jazzy Jaguar.

GEORGE B. GRAEN

Cincinnati, Ohio
July 1989

Acknowledgments

A nonfiction book about the secrets of how organizations work can only be as good as the career risks people share. I am indebted to the thousands of people and hundreds of companies who have let me share some of their often hard-learned secrets. They paid their dues, and I hope that we can learn from their successes and failures.

I am indebted to my mentors who taught me to look, question, look, sharpen my questions, look, and repeat this sequence until my sharpest questions revealed little more that was new. My father, Kelly Graen, used his questioning mind to waken my curiosity and keep me on my toes until Marv Dunnette and René Dawis, at the University of Minnesota, could add their unique perspectives to help me develop further. Later, at Illinois, Lloyd Humphreys, Ivan Steiner, and Joe McGrath contributed a wealth of skeptical substance, and Katsuo Sano introduced me to the Japanese style of skeptical inquiry. In Cincinnati, Phil Marvin and Milt Schloss taught me the gift of illuminating the executive's thought processes.

I am grateful to my research partners, Min Basadur, Mary Uhl Bien, Jim Cashman, Fred Dansereau, Jr., Steve Ginsburgh, Bill Haga, Thomas Johnson, Bob Liden, Takao Minami, Mike Novak, Dean Orris, Bill Schiemann, Anson Seers, Tim Serey, Patricia Sommerkamp, Mitsuru Wakabayashi, and John Weitzel. They taught me the secrets of close collaborative teamwork.

I am indebted to those who shared with me the emotional highs and lows of writing this book. My editor at John Wiley, John Mahaney, took the devil's advocate method to new heights, kept me from appearing the fool many times. My copyeditor, Shari Hatch, who showed me the forest when I was concentrating on the trees, made my rough ideas sing. My editorial assistants, who kept my attention on the book, Laurette Deubell, Doug Merritt, Terri Scandura, Adonis Vergara, Jr., and especially Mary Uhl Bien, never let me forget my audience. Clark Lawrence and Mitsuru Wakabayashi, who read my manuscripts, pushed me to reveal more than I intended.

Finally, closer to home, my sons, Mike and Marty, who let their dad try out his endless interpretations on them, never once showed impatience. Most of all, my wife Joni, who processed the ideas as well as the words through all of the revisions and is a living testimony to the vast power of human commitment, makes it all possible.

Contents

Foreword

Milton J. Schloss, Jr.
Retired Chairman & CEO, Sara Lee

Having spent more than 50 years in the business world, I have had to learn on the job many of the secrets of how organizations work. My preparation for management responsibilities started on the shop floor, performing the least skilled work, and I learned my way through progressively more skilled assignments. I learned the business from the bottom up, but most of the secrets described in this book were beyond merely knowing the business—these lessons required that I take some risks, learn about people, and work to help people achieve their own goals and the goals of the company at the same time.

One lesson I learned was that managers waste valuable resources when they don't invest in their people—one of the secrets described in this book. People make real contributions and enjoy their accomplishments so much more when they are helped to grow. This was a hard lesson for me to learn because I assumed that I must do everything myself and rely most heavily on my own talents. This book describes what I learned on the job: My people made me look good when I took the time to invest in them. In fact, the more I invested in them, the more my people came to use me as a resource. For example, my door was open to all of my people almost any time during the day, and they would drop in to bounce ideas and problems around. My role was to serve as a sounding board for ideas and problems. Often, small groups of managers and technical people from different areas would gather in my office to share their concerns and ideas. It was not unusual during these discussions to discover that a problem that one manager thought was unique to his or her area had implications for several different areas. My investment in the people I supervised was returned many times over.

Another lesson I learned was that some talented people devote too much time to negative actions. They criticize and complain about other people and the ways things are done in the company. They share their complaints with their co-workers, and the negativism spreads. It serves neither their interests nor those of their company. This is not a good way to get ahead. I favor the positive approach described throughout this book for confronting the many challenges of getting things accomplished in organizations. This approach instructs people to solve the problems that serve as barriers to effective performance rather than to curse the barriers. People can be the problem, or they can be the solution. A negative approach toward people sooner or later turns people into problems. In contrast, the positive approach described throughout this book tends to turn people into solutions.

I could have benefited by reading this book very early in my career. I still would have made my share of mistakes, but I certainly would have made far fewer. I recommend that people read this book and talk about it with their co-workers at many levels of the company. It is time that we share the secrets of how organizations work with everyone in our company—they must be on our team. Many of our foreign competitors are ahead of us in this. It gives them a competitive advantage that we cannot afford.

Foreword

MARVIN D. DUNNETTE
Professor of Psychology, The University of Minnesota
Founder, Personnel Decisions, Inc.,
and Personnel Decisions Research Institute

I have spent more than 30 years studying personnel decisions in organizations; over that time, I have also taught industrial and organizational psychology to many students. Nearly 50 of my students have obtained doctorates in psychology and have gone on to become teachers, scientists, practitioners, and organizational consultants. Among these talented scholars, a highly precocious student, Dr. George Graen, stood out. He has since spent more than 20 years studying organizations, which led to his writing the book you are now reading. I heartily commend its contents and congratulate you on your decision to read it.

In my work with students and with organizations, I seek ways for both students and organizations to maximize their intrinsic potential for success. I emphasize being straightforward—so much so that I am occasionally accused of being blunt. Thus, when helping organizations to reach their maximum levels of achievement and effectiveness, I have suggested a simple strategy for managers:

1. Set challenging but reachable goals.
2. Define clear pathways toward those goals.
3. Make explicit the operating rules for moving along the pathways.

4. Identify organizational sources of energy and strength that can be used efficiently, candidly, and wisely while proceeding toward the goals.

I had no label for this approach; it just seemed to match my own way of doing things. I now see that this strategy seems similar to aspects of the "unwritten rules" of organizational relationships and functioning that George Graen has described in his book. This information is crucial to organizational managers and other employees who seek to advance their own careers and to strengthen their own companies. However, because these unwritten rules are rarely made explicit, members of organizations must usually expend great effort to discover the rules—if they discover these rules at all.

In this book, Graen outlines the critical behind-the-scenes processes that effective managers and employees use to reach their goals, to build networks of competent co-workers, and to manage their careers. Graen's description of the unwritten rules reveals a hidden organization that is more orderly, more rational, and more predictable than the surface rules and structures of the visible organization. This understanding of the hidden organization both complements what is already known about organizational decision making and spells out promising new avenues of effective business practice. While reading, you may need to consider new ways of thinking about your career and your company. You will be well rewarded for doing so.

George Graen argues convincingly and tellingly that discovery of the unwritten rules of the hidden organization is critical for attaining both personal career success and organizational strength. With guidance and support from the ideas contained herein, organizational members throughout the hierarchy come to know the critical unwritten rules and thereby to gain those rewards that are contingent on this discovery.

UNWRITTEN RULES FOR YOUR CAREER

PART I

Seeking Success: Recognizing the Unwritten Rules

Why, When, and How to Learn Inside Information

Twenty years ago, Sun Publishing Company hired Juanita and John as technical writers. Today, Juanita earns $200,000 annually as the new CEO of Sun Publishing Corporation; John earns $40,000 annually as a senior technical writer there. Why was Juanita promoted more often and rewarded more generously than John? The answer is not easily found: She and John are equally intelligent, well educated, ambitious, and competent; they both keenly understand Sun's standard procedures for publishing. Yet Juanita clearly knows something or does something that John doesn't know or do. How did Juanita ride the fast track to success, leaving John behind? She had *inside information*: She had a firm grasp of the unwritten rules that govern organizations, and she used the hidden strategies suggested by those rules to manage her career.

Though Juanita and John are fictitious names, the theme of their stories is true. Most employees, like John, see only the organization's written policies, procedures, job descriptions, and other records.

These written rules reveal only the standard procedures and policies for handling routine tasks and staying in routine jobs. Rarely do they tell how to truly achieve in organizations. Meanwhile, insiders like Juanita discover the organization's *unwritten rules*—the undocumented operating rules that show how to handle exceptional circumstances and how to have an exceptional career.

Once they know the unwritten rules, insiders find out about the organization's *hidden strategies* for completing extraordinary projects and for handling difficult situations. These tactics are seldom even mentioned in meetings and are rarely found in written documents. But the insiders who discover these tactics use their knowledge of the unwritten rules and the hidden strategies to perform vital tasks in their organizations. Thus, discovery and use of this inside information decisively advances both the careers of the insiders and the interests of the organizations they serve. Organizations increasingly seek and reward these insiders, moving them along the fast track to success.

What You Gain by Learning the Inside Information

A few insiders know how to get what they want from the organization, but they choose not to take management positions. However, they still enjoy numerous benefits from their insider information:

• Expert yet stress-free competence
• Esteem from and influence with peers and supervisors
• Access to resources and perquisites

How to Learn the Inside Information

Many insiders had learned about the unwritten rules and the hidden strategies from family and friends who were on the fast track themselves. Other fast-trackers have learned these secrets the hard way—through their own mistakes. But you need not risk stumbling onto these the hard way—or worse, risk never finding them at all, remaining forever tied to the slow track. You now have the chance to find out the inside information from this book. Once you've learned how to find out the unwritten rules and hidden strategies, you can easily grasp and thoughtfully apply them. You can light your own path to the fast track.

This book is intended to open the fast track to those of you who seek to work productively in your organization and who expect to harvest the fruits of your labor. If you strive to become the best you can be, you can find here the vehicles to ride to the fast track. This book allows you to steer your sleek sportscar onto the fast track.

1

Discover 15 Secrets of the Fast Track

The Importance of Secrets

Secrets abound in all organizations, no matter what their size or industry. Some secrets are unique to the organization or industry that keeps them. Others apply across the broad spectrum of organizations and industries. Even Mom-and-Pop businesses have developed many unwritten routines and hidden procedures for handling work. This inside information rarely creates problems for Mom and Pop because they're both insiders. If unexpected changes arise, they can solve the problems without too much difficulty: Mom and Pop sit down and figure out what to do. Inside information only creates problems if Mom and Pop aren't around when the information is needed.

In other organizations, this inside information can create tremendous problems—both for the organizations and for the people who work in them. When anything happens that falls outside the written policies and standard routines, people who lack the inside information become completely ineffective in getting things done. If they're lucky, they may eventually be able to jerry-build an adequate way of handling the situation. If they're not, they fail miserably. This clearly harms both the people and the organization. In our present age of rampant technological innovation and a rapidly changing international marketplace, we must increasingly expect the unexpected.

So why do organizations have secrets if secrets have such harmful effects? Most secrets evolve innocently enough: It's usually impossible to keep up with the tremendous amount of activity and change that's constantly going on in and around any organization. No one could possibly write down everything that everyone really does in an organization—and no one would read it if someone could.

Further, some organizational secrets exist for the same reason that personal secrets do: to protect people from hearing things that will make them feel sad, mad, or otherwise bad. You may know that Judy isn't as good a typist as Ed, but you don't say so to Judy. You may wish that your boss was as effective a manager as the head of the sales division, but you don't rush in to say that to your boss. Your supervisor certainly has feelings about the relative merits of the people in your unit. But you probably won't hear what those feelings are even though *your career is being affected by those feelings*.

You need not know *all* of your organization's inside information—much of it has no bearing on your career. But you must know some of these secrets if you are to succeed. This chapter reveals 15 of these vital secrets that your organization, like most organizations, may be concealing from you. These eye-openers will show you how to think about your career in a new way, giving you more control over your own career. Later chapters describe how you can use this inside information to manage your career and guide it onto the fast track.

The 15 Secrets

All of the secrets in this chapter relate to what some people call "political behavior" in organizations. To function effectively in any organization, you must understand these political behaviors. Right now, many of your organization's political secrets are playing a decisive role in your career. Once you understand them, you can use them to achieve your own objectives, as well as those of your organization. The inside information about political behaviors described in this chapter relates to the following topics:

1. Searching for the inside
2. Inside homework and inside tests
3. Taking risks
4. Flexible planning
5. Insider's view of compensation
6. Promotion from the inside
7. Ensuring mutual promotion
8. Insider networks
9. Specialist traps
10. Inside foresight
11. Cordial competition
12. Multiple mentors
13. Distribution of credit
14. Equivalent exchanges
15. Reputation for fairness

Secret 1. Searching for the Inside

Find the Hidden Strategies of Your Organization, and Use Them to Achieve Your Objectives. Written rules and explicit procedures constitute only one facet of your organization's operational guidelines and functional strategies. I call these written rules and overt procedures the organization's "public mask." This mask may be fine for describing the company to outsiders, but as a prescription for effective actions in managerial or professional jobs, it is woefully inadequate.

Go beyond these explicit prescriptions, and learn to uncover how things really get done in your organization. There are two fundamental ways to learn how to find the hidden strategies for effective action on new and unanticipated problems: Initially, you must discover them through trial and error; later learning comes from observing the experiences of others.

There appear to be three kinds of learners: (1) people who don't learn from their experiences and are doomed to repeat mistakes; (2) people who learn from their experiences but get scarred in the process; and (3) people who learn from the experiences of others. Become aware of the kind of learning you do now, and determine whether you need to try a new approach.

Don't let a day go by in which you don't investigate what really goes on and how work really gets done in your organization. Continually observe, ask questions, listen, and learn. To begin charting the hidden strategies in your organization, pay heed to how tasks are assigned. For example, you may need to work collaboratively with others to complete a project. Your boss may have alluded to some of the differences between the explicit strategies—the way things *should be done* according to the organization's overt communications—and the *hidden strategies*—the way things *actually are done*. However, you alone must discover the particular hidden strategies that relate to your project.

In the process of completing this project, you begin to experience the true power of organizations: *working relationships*—that is, forming collaborative relationships among people with special resources, skills, or abilities, to do important work. Those who have developed and maintained collaborative networks of working relationships wield tremendous organizational power, regardless of their official title and rank in the organization. These networks of working relationships are critical components of the unwritten rules and hidden strategies of your organization. They provide the flexibility required to deal with unanticipated events, often even contradicting the explicit rules and procedures of the organization's public mask. The following example illustrates the inherent power of these networks.

> Joan Martin's company was under a strict hiring freeze, and no one could be hired without approval from the president of the company—a process that could have taken several months. In Joan's department of six people, suddenly two people left for personal reasons. She had been just barely meeting deadlines with six people, and now she had to do the same amount of work with four. Immediately, she requested emergency relief from the freeze, but it was denied. She next asked for permission to hire two people and was told it may take from two to three months to go through the procedure. She and her boss searched for peo-

ple to transfer to her department and found none. The explicit tactics of the public mask had failed her. She was not meeting deadlines, and her work was backlogged. Her department had become the bottleneck of the entire division.

Finally, she asked her network of co-workers to help her. Two managers not in Joan's division came to her rescue. These managers were the major customers of the work done in Joan's department, and Joan had helped both of them in the past. They chided Joan for not coming to them sooner and proceeded to make informal arrangements to transfer some of Joan's work to their people and to prioritize the work they needed from Joan's department. As a result, some work was done by people in these two other departments, and some low-priority work was shelved for completion after the freeze. In this way, Joan was able to weather the freeze without harm to her career.

If Joan had not been saved by these two managers, she would have experienced a major failure. Fortunately, Joan had established good working relationships with these two colleagues by collaborating with them when they needed her help. This collaboration across organizational division lines appeared on no company document; it is part of the secret organization within Joan's company. If Joan had followed only the explicit tactics of her organization, her colleagues would not have been able to save her. The test of any such network is whether people are there when you really need them.

You must discover and chart the hidden strategies of your organization if you are serious about advancing your career. Once you diagram these strategies, your chart can provide you with reliable direction and guidance. Remember also to adapt it to respond to new problems and to update it to keep it current.

Though you have started to chart the hidden strategies of your organization, continue to keep track of the explicit strategies of the public mask. Note when it is more appropriate to follow the explicit strategies, as opposed to the hidden ones you are discovering. For ordinary, routine jobs, following the explicit strategies may be the most prudent approach. Try also to be sensitive to the views of

Exercise. Job Description: Explicit Versus Hidden

As soon as possible, get a copy of your own job description,* and read it over. Underline the things on it that you do often or that really make a difference in how well you do your job. Draw a line through those things that you seldom do and that make very little difference to how well you do your job.

Now, on a separate sheet of paper, make a list of all the things you do often or that are important to your success in your job, but *aren't* listed in your job description. Do you help your boss to write reports? Do you handle client calls when others are at lunch? Do you help train newcomers? Once you've thought of all you can think of, ask some of your co-workers to help you think of other things to add to your list. Keep the list handy at your desk, and add or delete things as you notice them. You can write your own "unwritten rules."

Be thinking about

- Which tasks you'd like to outgrow that are on the list
- Which tasks you need to master more successfully if you are to outgrow your present job
- What tasks you don't see on the list but would like to grow into

You'll use this list in Chapter 5, "Outgrow Your Present Job."

*If you don't already have a job description, write a list of

- Things you do that you would like to do less (that you don't enjoy)
- Things you do that you'd like to continue doing (don't mind doing)
- Things you do that you'd like to do more (enjoy doing)
- Things you'd like to do that you aren't doing now (would enjoy doing)

people in your organization who do not yet perceive the value of the hidden strategies and who resent your use of them.

Some may suggest that the hidden strategies are subversive and chaotic. Don't offend valuable co-workers trying to convince them otherwise. Instead, maintain your own focus on what strategies will be the most appropriate and effective both for long-term working relationships and for the situation at hand. Remember that the co-workers whom you may consider alienating by hastily implementing the hidden strategies may be just the people you'll later need to complete a crucial project. You'll more easily sway them with collaborative successes than with competitive defeats.

Secret 2. Inside Homework and Inside Tests

Do Your Homework in Order to Pass the Tests. You will be tested in many different ways by many different people, but not all tests have career relevance. The tests that you must pass are unlike those that you took in school: They are not announced as tests, they are subjectively evaluated, and you may never be told the results. Tests range from a simple, apparently innocent question to a professional command performance. You may be tested by anyone at any rank at any time. Moreover, the career relevance of your performance does not depend on the title or rank of your evaluator. This may seem unfair to students who have lived much of their lives in the artificial world of the classroom, but it is appropriate within the hidden realm of the organization.

In turn, you must also learn to test those with whom you interact. Unless you evaluate the sources of your information, you cannot evaluate the quality of the information derived. If you neglect to do this, you may unwittingly transmit information of unknown quality, thus committing a grave error in judgment.

To evaluate information effectively, get it from a variety of sources. Don't limit your own perspective to the narrow views of only one other person. If you gather information from many sources, you can more easily judge the information's truthfulness and its validity. Also don't assume that a majority view is correct. Sometimes, the minority sees things more clearly or has access to information unavailable to others.

Information, however, isn't all you need from others. Within an organization, you generally must depend on others to accomplish your tasks, and the quality of your work depends on the quality of others' work. Hence, you must evaluate the work of others or you risk being responsible for poor quality or low productivity. When the quality of others' work is unacceptable, you must find ways to bring it up to standard and beyond. Although a flaw in a project that you share may technically be the fault of someone else, you should take responsibility for it and correct it. This is one way of outgrowing the restrictive confines of your present job.

Secret 3. Taking Risks

Accept Calculated Risks by Using Appropriate Contingency Plans. To advance in your career, you must be willing to take career risks as a way of life. You must also be ready to accept the consequences of the risks you take. While preparing yourself to deal with the possible consequences of your decision, consider the precautions you might take in order to minimize the potential for damaging results.

The *decision average* is the average of the number of good decisions in relation to the total number of decisions (like the batting average in baseball). Though no statistician formally tracks these averages, many people track them informally. Various interested others may disagree about how to define a wise decision, but whatever their definition, they calculate your decision average. As with baseball, the people with lower averages must be defensive specialists or have some other valued skill; those with higher averages are stars; and those with the highest averages are superstars.

Your goal should be to improve your decision average by taking calculated risks that lead to increasingly realistic decisions. If you decide not to make a decision—to let others make it for you or to let the situation continue until it dictates the decision— recognize that you are still facing risks. Choosing not to make a decision, or to postpone a decision indefinitely means simply that you are making a decision by default. If this is your decision, you have decided *not* to manage or guide your career—a very big risk indeed. In terms of the fast track, avoiding career risks may be the riskiest alternative of all.

As an insider, you'll learn to improve your decision average by taking career risks. Of course, you'll make some mistakes and take some missteps, but you'll learn from them and move forward. What's more, you'll be able to savor the outcomes of decisions that prove prudent, whereas nondecision decisions, even when the outcome is positive, offer little true satisfaction.

Secret 4. Flexible Planning

Recognize that Apparently Complete and Final Plans Are Merely Flexible Guidelines to the Actions Necessary for Implementation. Although plans are useful tools for directing coordinated actions, they can only provide a framework for decision making during their implementation. For all but the simplest plan, the turbulence in the implementation situation requires that additional decisions be made and unanticipated actions be taken to make the plan work in the real world.

A realistic approach to planning is to devise a plan that is neither overly vague and open to misinterpretation nor overly specific and closed to adaptation. An overly specific, inflexible plan may work perfectly in the simplified microworld of the computer simulation but fail abysmally in the real world. Or a plan that is too general and ambiguous may fail utterly to guide and coordinate actions. Somewhere between these two extremes lie the workable alternatives for a trade-off between thoroughness and flexibility in a plan. Make your plans broad and open-ended enough to allow easy adaptation in the implementation process. But provide enough specific suggestions for action to give clear instructions that are easily followed.

> Biggs, a French firm, had a plan to establish the largest discount food and department store in the world. Their marketing plan called for economies of scale in purchasing and minimum prices to consumers. They selected the home office city (Cincinnati) of one of the largest grocery corporations in the United States (Kroger's) as the site for their first store. However, they made no provisions for adapting French ownership to suit U.S. employees.
>
> Although their plan worked well on paper, this store failed to achieve the large profits they had expected. A new manager was hired to make the store profitable. He changed the philosophy of the store from one of subordinate domestic employees directed by foreign managers to one of teamwork and individual responsibility. Under the new concept, everyone was a team player responsible for the performance of the store. All the team members were asked to make the store more effective and efficient by improving

their work. To bolster the team's commitment to the store, the manager established a profit-sharing plan under which all team members shared in success.

Many small changes were made under this program. Some worked and some didn't, but they continued to experiment. The results were gratifying. The store became profitable and continues to be so. The problem with the original plan was that it was both incomplete and unresponsive to the new locale. Success depended on modifying the plan in order to motivate the employees to go beyond the plan and improve the way they accomplished their objectives. Employees discovered how to work together more effectively, but they needed to be allowed to make improvements and to be given a real incentive. Because the new store manager accomplished his goals, he was next given the assignment of making a second new store equally profitable.

No one can design plans that function perfectly in the dynamic real world of business. Sometimes your rules and procedures will be overdone, and sometimes they will be underdone. Even the most sophisticated computers can only devise plans that work well in the narrow constraints of a computer simulation. In the wider world of unpredictable events, too many things can happen that you cannot anticipate in advance. The best that you can do is to give people some guidelines and some latitude for action to deal with events that you cannot anticipate. Try as you might, you cannot write rules and procedures to cover every possible contingency. Instead, specify clear objectives, and provide guidelines for people to modify the plans in order to deal with events as they occur. Moreover, when implementing plans—your own or those of others—you'll learn to add new rules and procedures and to modify established ones. Whenever possible, delete rules and procedures that no longer serve their purpose.

Secret 5. Insider's View of Compensation

Expect to be Financially Undercompensated for the First Half of Your Career and to be Overcompensated for the Second Half. As an American, you expect to receive *equitable compensation*, which assures a relative equality of value between what you contribute to your organization and what compensation you receive from your organization. However, formal reward systems cannot keep pace with the rapid increases in the contributions of fast-trackers early in their careers. Because such people quickly grow out of their entry jobs by taking on extra job duties and responsibilities before they are officially promoted, they frequently do much more than they are paid to do. If you view this period of inequity from a short-term perspective, you may feel cheated or exploited by the organization. As a result, you may be tempted to reduce your contributions to reach the low level of your compensation. This would be a mistake.

Instead of viewing equity short-sightedly, in terms of your current situation, try to view equity from a career-long perspective. This perspective may help you to avoid feeling cheated when you notice temporary inequity of compensation when you are doing more than you are paid to do. If you let yourself fall into this trap, you erect barriers to keep yourself off the fast track in your organization. Although you may occasionally feel that your efforts are not fully appreciated by your boss—most people do—don't give in to these feelings by cutting back on your career investment. Rather, by taking a far-sighted view of your career, you can avoid the impulse to rectify the imbalance in the current situation. Keep your focus on your long-term career goals, and continue to do more than you are currently being paid to do. You'll be abundantly rewarded later in your career.

This principle remains valid even when organizations are restructuring and cutting back the size of their staffs. The people who are identified for outplacement in such restructuring plans typically are those who are not on the fast track. People on the fast track have invested in the organization by growing out of their job descriptions and doing more than they were paid to do ("sweat equity"). They are recognized as people who continue to invest and are expected to invest in the future. In fact, they are counted on to make the restructuring plan succeed. Moreover, the organization recognizes that it has invested in the careers of these people through development and support over the years. These investments by the organization may not appear on any document, but when staff is reduced, this information plays a decisive role.

You must, however, be sensible. Don't wait to look for life preservers until the waves splash your ankles on the sinking ship.

Discreetly investigate other options while continuing to be productive on your present job. Your boss is investing in you for long-term benefits, and you must also invest in yourself for the long term. Short-term thinking by either party tends to be detrimental to the full blossoming of your potential. Any investment requires risks in order to derive future benefits. Both you and your boss must assume your respective share of the present risks to reap future profits. The critical role of mutual trust is discussed in Secrets 7 and 14.

Secret 6. Promotion from the Inside

Work to Make Your Boss Successful. If your boss is successful, your boss gains prestige and power. If you are instrumental in making your boss successful, you are likely to gain as well. Thus, both you and your boss may outgrow your present jobs. If nothing else, your unit will demonstrate its worth, and its requests for resources will be well received.

One way to begin to promote your boss effectively is to discuss with your boss what you need to provide in order for your boss to be effective. Ask your boss the following kinds of questions:

• What information do you need?

• What are the sensitive areas that you want monitored carefully?

• How can I help you to make the work unit more productive?

Questions such as these show your boss that you are committed to making your boss more effective and that you are concerned with a larger picture than your present job.

If you offer to take on assignments that are outside of your job, be prepared to perform them competently. Taking on such assignments requires that you ask your boss for the additional resources needed to do the assignment. Although you shouldn't expect to be relieved of your duties or given more time, you should ask for support and guidance from your boss. If needed, ask for permission to use your boss's authority. Don't be too timid to request the resources you need to finish the assignment. If your boss suggested that you ask for resources as needed, ask for them. If you do not use appropriate resources on such assignments, you are not likely to be successful, which will not help promote your boss. Also, requesting appropriate help for completing a task reminds your boss that you are performing these extra assignments. It requires your boss to invest in you while you are making your investment.

Promoting your boss goes to the heart of the exchange between you and your boss. Unless you develop an attitude of empathizing with your boss and doing what is good for your boss's career, the process can be truncated. Remember that bosses are managing their own careers as well as those of subordinates. Bosses tend to be more receptive to the needs of subordinates who are understanding and readily reciprocate for this assistance. By working to promote your boss, you may increase the influence of your boss and, consequently, your own opportunities for career development.

One of the greatest threats to the full blossoming of a collaborative relationship is narrow, short-term self-interested thinking by either party. When either party focuses too narrowly on immediate personal payoffs, the growth of the exchange is affected adversely. Both parties will share the outcome of this exchange, and the finished product must be greater than the sum of its respective parts. Anything you do to improve the result will ultimately benefit you.

You might think of this as if you and your boss are baking a cake together: Neither of you can bake alone—each has essential ingredients. If one party withholds essential ingredients, the cake will almost certainly be less palatable to both of you; it may even be inedible. Moreover, once you and your boss have baked your first cake and tasted the results, you may be encouraged to invest even more of your time and energy and produce more delectable fare. You'll learn more about baking, and you'll develop your skills in the process. The collaborative process expands the scope of the exchange. Success breeds success.

You should also promote your boss in other ways: If you help your boss to rise quickly, you can easily rise in your boss's slipstream, thus reducing resistance to your swift movement upward. You may discover previously unknown or unexplored ways to increase your boss's achievements. If you become alert to the opportunities and threats to your boss's productivity, you can act to promote your boss's success.

For example, your boss may not know about a career opportunity or may be in need of some moral support to accept a challenging assignment. Alert your boss to opportunities and encourage your boss to accept challenges. Clearly, you are most valuable to your boss when you are dependable and supportive.

By putting the interests of your boss first, you increase the value of your boss's investment in you, and vice versa. This reciprocal nature of promotion is one of the best-kept secrets of management.

Secret 7. Ensuring Mutual Promotion

Work to Get Your Boss to Promote Your Career. When you promote your boss's career, you may reasonably expect that your boss will reciprocate and promote your career. If this expectation is fulfilled by a knowledgeable boss, you both work to make each other more effective and hence more promotable. However, if your boss does not fulfill this expectation after a suitable period of time, you must devise a way for your boss to complete the reciprocal half of the exchange. One-way streets quickly become dead ends and are unused. Only two-way streets are maintained for long.

To get your boss both to understand the two-way exchange and to begin promoting your career, simply discuss what you need to do your work effectively. By discussing what you need, you focus attention on the other half of the exchange. Whether you schedule a meeting or take your boss to lunch, be sure to have this conversation. Chapter 3 describes how to tell whether your boss already considers you to be on the fast track.

One of the most straightforward ways of getting promoted in organizations is by outgrowing your present job and grooming your replacement. To do this quickly usually takes the active collaboration of your boss. To be promoted, you need help to know what you must learn, and you need opportunities to learn it. In this way, you and your boss reciprocally work to promote one another. By this process, both you and your boss can develop professionally and become fast-trackers. Part II (especially Chapter 4) explains how to get onto and stay on the fast track.

Superiors and subordinates who build two-way streets also develop effective working relationships that often mature into career-long professionally supportive relationships. In building these relationships, both parties invest over and above that required by their jobs. They both outgrow their jobs in terms of doing more for each other and for the organization.

Nonetheless, neither your boss nor this book can put you on the fast track. You must be motivated to take charge of your own career, take the initiative in outgrowing your present job, and take the reins as you move to the fast track. Before leading others, you must show that you can guide your own career.

Be sure also to remember this mutuality of interests when you are the boss. Part III describes more fully how to lead as an insider.

Once you develop effective working relationships with your boss, you may find that some co-workers accuse you of being a "brown-noser." A brown-noser is someone who gets better treatment from the boss through ingratiation alone and has not earned it. Though you may feel hurt by this accusation, rest assured that you have worked hard to build a reciprocal relationship and that you have earned everything you receive from your boss.

People who do not understand the secret strategies of how organizations function sometimes perceive those who do understand it and capitalize on it as not playing by the rules. They may falsely accuse fast-trackers of benefiting from favoritism. But favoritism is the practice of giving resources based on personal attraction only. Clearly, the strategies suggested here involve much more substantial returns for a boss's favors. Instead of becoming hurt or angry when your co-workers misunderstand your actions, try to understand their envy and their frustration. When appropriate, you may even encourage them in their careers as well. The process of building reciprocal relationships of mutual effort is a highly ethical, if poorly understood, route to the fast track.

All working relationships in organizational units are not equally effective. Some are two-way, high-quality superhighways; some are two-way streets; and some are dead-end streets. Even within the same unit, these three kinds of relationships may exist. It is not unusual for some bosses to have all three kinds within their units. People clearly on the fast track usually build two-way, superhighway relationships with their bosses. As they move rapidly up the organization, they build such high-quality two-way relationships at each step on the ladder. These reciprocal relationships offer you a competitive advantage in your career development. Not everyone can be on the fast track. The difference between those who are and those who aren't often comes down to knowing a little more about how the organization really works.

Secret 8. Insider Networks

Use Reciprocal Relationships to Build Supportive Networks. Each
time you are assigned to a new work unit, you add new connections
to a growing network of support. As you establish these reciprocal
links, over and above your job responsibilities with your current
key co-workers, you further enhance your effectiveness and your
promotability. Each new reciprocal link adds to your network of
effective working relationships with competent others. Such *competence networks* allow you first to move to the fast track and later to
stay on it. These networks prodigiously multiply your effectiveness,
and they can make possible otherwise infeasible projects. Competence networks are described more fully in Chapter 6.

Secret 9. Specialist Traps

Don't Let Your Areas of Competence Become Too Narrowly Specialized. Career opportunities tend to grow at a geometric rate once
you implement the collaborative process with your boss. However,
you must actively search for true professional challenges. Even with
collaboration, you may become an indispensable technician in a
specialty area and become stuck for too long in one job; this is the
specialist trap. You can avoid this specialist trap through continually
assuming new and different professional challenges.

Avoiding the specialist trap is not easy. Once you develop competence in a specialty, it is difficult to leave the safe shelter of competence for the risk of challenging new assignments. It may be
comfortable to hide behind well-learned skills, and it is often quite
uncomfortable to struggle to master new ones. But you must continue to develop professionally. Accepting new challenges is not
always fun: It is hard work and often painful. Although the mastery
of new skills can be satisfying, the acquisition of these skills can be
misery.

The importance of avoiding the specialist trap can't be overemphasized in the rapidly changing world of business. Look in the
white pages of your phone book; find all the Smiths and Chandlers.
Now flip to the yellow pages to find out how many blacksmiths and
candle-makers are employed—regardless of how competent they

are. Being the best specialist in an obsolete field is *not* the way to the fast track.

Throughout your career, you must periodically face a dilemma:

• Remain in a safely mastered specialty, enjoying feelings of confidence, security, and esteem—but trapped by your own competence.

• Accept new challenges and trials, experiencing doubt and risking humiliation—but free to rise to greater heights.

Such career decisions are difficult, but you must make them. The nature of the managerial fast track is one of confronting such impossible choices. You will rarely make perfect decisions, but somehow you must decide.

Your boss may readily offer you new challenges, but sometimes you must actively pursue them. However, don't make your boss think you're impatient or that you mistrust your boss's judgment. Your career could be ruined by taking on more than you can handle or by alienating your boss.

Secret 10. Inside Foresight

Try to Act with Foresight More Often than with Hindsight. Foresighted *proaction* is action based on an educated anticipation of how events will happen. As in chess, the proactive player thinks about tactics several moves in advance and tries to anticipate the opponent's tactics. In contrast, *reaction* is an isolated response to a single event. In chess, the reactive player responds only to each of the opponent's moves. Proaction involves looking beyond the present and attempting to anticipate how events will unfold, with the aim of capitalizing on opportunities and avoiding, or at least minimizing, threats.

Proaction requires that you find out how things really work in your organization. In this way, you can anticipate problems and solve them even before they become serious crises. There appear to be three phases of effective proaction:

1. Identify the right potential problem.
2. Find the right solution to avert the problem.

3. Choose the best process for implementing the solution to the problem.

Within each phase of the process, you follow three steps: (1) generate alternatives, (2) evaluate the alternatives, and (3) select an alternative. These phases and steps are described more fully in Chapter 7, "Solve Problems."

When you use this three-phase system, you assume the risk that you might be wrong; over time, however, competently using the proactive system improves your decision average more than the reactive system. One key reason that proactive decisions are usually superior to reactive decisions is that with proaction, you can take the time to gather more diverse information and to think of more alternatives than when you must reactively respond to a crisis. Once you are in a crisis, you cannot afford to take the time to be proactive. Clearly, proaction cannot be used for all decisions or in all situations. Those decisions or situations that require immediate response do not allow the luxury of proactive decision making. Follow the basic rule of timing in decision making: "Never make a decision until you absolutely must, but be ready to make it on a moment's notice."

Being proactive also encourages you to gather information from people who know what they're doing. Instead of jealously protecting your proprietary decision-making responsibility, seek quality information and insights from other competent people regardless of their position or rank. Don't allow yourself to get trapped in a narrow point of view; to generate a wide variety of high-quality alternatives, seek out multiple perspectives. Chapter 7 ("Solve Problems") shows how to break away from a limited perspective.

Secret 11. Cordial Competition

Develop **Cordial** *Relationships with Your Competitors: Be Courteous, Considerate, and Polite in All Relationships.* But don't mistake consideration for weakness, and don't confuse politeness with affection. Developing effective work relationships requires that you use your entire range of social interaction styles when dealing with people.

On the one hand, you need to learn to be cordial with both co-operators and competitors. You need not like the the people with whom you're cordial. But simple social courtesies go a long way in maintaining positive working relationships. If you cannot be cordial, you are trapped into being nasty, rude, and thoughtless.

On the other hand, you must learn to be tough—or even abrasive—when the situation calls for standing firm and asserting your own work-related values. Toughness means that you must be able to ask the hard questions and give the hard answers when required. You must especially be ready to admit your mistakes candidly. Often you must be pushy or unyielding on your own projects. If you cannot be tough, you are trapped into being pushed around by people tougher than you.

Of the thousands of managers in almost every type of organization, those who can demonstrate a variety of social interaction styles, drawing on the full range of emotions, tend to be the most effective. I call these people "cordial tough guys." Such people are typically cordial (courteous and considerate) to all who interact with them; however, when they need to ask the hard question or give the hard answer they can do so forcefully.

In contrast, the "cordial pushover" tends to be cordial regardless of the situation and tends to avoid hard questions and hard answers. "Pollyanna" may be an alternative label for this more limited style of interacting. These people perform best in situations that require few hard decisions or actions. They appear to be incapable of urging people to correct their errors or to improve their work.

In sharp contrast, some live their entire professional lives on the dark side—the "nasty tough guy." "Nasty tough guys" can make the tough decisions and ask the hard questions, but their lack of cordiality makes them ineffective. They are unable to build collaborative working relationships because they don't know how to be cordial.

Finally, the "nasty pushover" is the worst of both worlds. This person is neither cordial enough to build collaborative working relationships nor tough enough to make sure things get done. Working relationships with either of the nasty types can be emotionally taxing. However, the nasty tough guy is more likely to be effective than the nasty pushover, especially if the nasty tough guy is a technical expert. The nasty pushover tends to be almost invisible in organizations, with an office away from the flow of people and often hidden in the bowels of the building.

Developing cordial working relationships with competitors can

pay dividends later. Over time, competitors usually become coop-
erators and supportive colleagues. Clearly, cordial competitors come
and go, but enemies seldom forget. You will make enough enemies
in the course of getting things done without adding unnecessarily
to the list through nasty encounters. Simply being the tough guy
when appropriate tends to make enemies. But making enemies unnecessarily by being nasty can be an expensive luxury that your
career can't afford.

Secret 12. Multiple Mentors

Seek Out Key Expert Insiders, and Learn from Them. During a manager's career, many different mentors prove helpful. Each mentor
has something to teach. At each stage of your career development,
seek out appropriate mentors. You may learn from a mentor as a
result of a formal program or in some less formal process. Once you
learn how to learn from mentors, you can learn with a variety of
different people. The underlying process will be similar, though the
particular characteristics of the parties, their behaviors, and the context may differ.

One potential problem that you must learn to handle, however,
is how to make the transition from one mentor to another. The
problem of switching mentors requires special efforts on your part.
Without careful attention, the previous mentor may feel betrayed
and used. You can, however, avoid this problem by carefully preparing for the transition. Although you must move on with your
career, you must leave as graciously and amicably as possible. Pre-
serve the valuable working relationships you worked so hard to
cultivate. Maintain the reciprocal links of your professional network.

Secret 13. Distribution of Credit

Make Sure to Acknowledge Everyone's Contribution. Being generous with credit does not diminish your contribution. In most organizations, many valuable contributions are seldom acknowledged.
Most people do more than they are paid to do. Though a few do

less, most do more. Hence, most people are pleasantly surprised when their contribution is recognized and appreciated.

When people do something beyond the call of duty for you, even if they don't expect any acknowledgment, learn to give them credit. The next time you are in need, they may remember and reciprocate. People who are stingy in giving credit are making a mistake. Credit is a valued commodity in organizations; it tends to grow when invested in others and to shrink when guarded too closely.

Professional credit can be used as a tool to develop a network of working relationships. Effective managers make certain that everyone's contribution to the success of a project is publicly acknowledged. When many technicians contribute to technical devices or processes, effective managers carefully note the name and contribution of each technician, making sure that such contributions are acknowledged. Future contributions are more generously given when past contributions are appreciated. Too often, individual contributions go unrecognized.

Though you are the one person most interested in your own career, you must still remember to promote the careers of the competent others who help you succeed. Don't limit your view to those above you in the organization. Be sure also to focus on the contributions of those at your own rung or those below you on the career ladder.

Secret 14. Equivalent Exchanges

Prefer Equivalent Exchanges Between Peers Instead of Rewards and Punishments Between Unequal Partners. An *equivalent exchange* is a transaction in which a resource (such as information), a service (such as typing), or a behavior (such as expression of concern) is given, with the understanding that a resource, service, or behavior of equivalent value will eventually be returned. On the other hand, providing or withholding rewards or punishment to shape the behavior of others assumes that the provider of rewards and punishments has superior power over the recipient, in that the recipient is in some way dependent on the resources (rewards or punishments) of the provider. This dependency is most potent when the recipient needs the particular resources, and the provider is the only source available. Thus, the working relationship is one in which the recipient is made subordinate to the provider.

Thus, the predominant feature of relationships based on rewards and punishments is inequity and lack of trust: "I can't trust you to want to be fair, so I must constantly dole out rewards and mete out punishments to keep you in line." On the other hand, equitable relationships, based on equivalent exchanges, assume trustworthiness among the participants: "I am giving this to you now because I know that you want to be fair, and I can assume that you will eventually return to me something of equivalent value."

Using rewards and punishments to influence behavior can actually harm the development of effective working relationships because this strategy forces the recipient to be dependent on the provider. For some interactions, in the early stages in a working relationship, this might be appropriate. However, as a relationship matures, both parties should be increasingly competent and independent, so rewards and punishments become less and less appropriate. Once a working relationship matures beyond this primitive stage, direct rewards and punishments tend to be insulting and demeaning.

In the more mature stages of a working relationship, as the two parties get to know each other, sometimes as soon as within a few weeks, the transactions become equivalent exchanges. Behavior of your boss is exchanged for your behavior; resources of your boss are exchanged for your resources; sentiments of your boss are reciprocated for your sentiments; and vice versa. This equivalent exchange does not assume a one-way dependency relationship. It does assume a collaborative one in which the exercise of unequal power has no place.

For example, your boss may help (behavior) you with a difficult assignment, and you will find some appropriate way (behavior) to reciprocate this kindness. You should not attempt to exchange resources for behavior because to do so would be insulting (in the nature of an impersonal payment for services rendered). In mature working relationships, be they superior-to-subordinate or peer-to-peer, people make exchanges of equivalent value. They reciprocate behavior for behavior, resources for resources, and sentiments for sentiments.

Mature working relationships tend to cease developing and plateau when the next higher level of sentiments, resources, and behaviors are not reciprocated. Another characteristic of mature working relationships is that both parties build credit with each other so that equivalent exchanges may be delayed for a considerable period of time without injurious consequences. Early in the development of the relationship, before much of this credit is established, these equivalent exchanges cannot be delayed very long without negative effects. But when mutual trust and support develop, the delay of exchange can be tolerated. At this point, neither party is concerned that the other will take unfair advantage. Methods of building such mature working relationships are described in Chapter 6.

Secret 15. Reputation for Fairness

Never Take Unfair Advantage of Anyone, and Avoid Letting Anyone Take Unfair Advantage of You. You must live in the small community of co-workers. Either you earn and maintain a reputation for honest and open dealings, or you suffer the dire consequences. The key to effectiveness in organizations is developing a network of high-quality working relationships, and each of the working relationships in your network must be based on trust.

If you fail to develop a reputation as a person who can be trusted or you develop a reputation as a person who cannot be trusted, the network you need either will not materialize or will disintegrate. Your career has limited potential if this happens. To develop mature working relationships, your potential partner and you must take professional risks. Require assurance from others that they are trustworthy, and ensure your own reputation for fair and open transactions. This makes the mutual risks acceptable.

Your reputation is your bond in developing working relationships. Your reputation has two dimensions: (1) whether you would take unfair advantage of someone else, and (2) whether you would let someone else take unfair advantage of you. Both of these dimensions are important in the calculation of trust: The first demonstrates your professional fairness and the second shows your prudence. In other words, you *can* be too trusting of others. Gullibility can be as damaging as treachery to the development of new working relationships. Not everyone can be trusted equally, and you must test others even as you are tested for trust.

Protect and nurture carefully your professional reputation: It is a priceless asset that follows you from organization to organization throughout your career.

Summary

Organizations can be described in at least two different ways. I call the most obvious descriptions the "public mask," shown in the many written rules and procedures of the company. In contrast, quite a different description of an organization, which I call the "hidden face," is understood only through on-the-job experiences that reveal the hidden strategies and unwritten rules of the organization. The difference between the public mask and the hidden face is the difference between how a document claims that a task should be done and how an insider actually does it. Understanding the inside information can give you a competitive advantage in your career relative to those who only follow the dictates of the public mask. The next chapter discusses the unwritten rules and how to read them in your organization.

2

Read the Unwritten Rules

Professional business schools rarely prepare people to become insiders—to unmask the hidden face of organizations, to discover the unwritten rules and covert strategies for being successful within the organization. Instead, most schools show students only the public mask of organizations' written documentation and overt practices. Unfortunately, when business-school graduates join organizations, they experience situations that make no sense when viewed in terms of the written policies and the public-mask tactics of their organizations. They feel frustrated by these apparent contradictions, and they complain to confidants that management professes one set of rules but operates by another.

To adapt to these inconsistencies, people develop coping mechanisms. Some of them try to discover the underlying rules by observing what seems to work. They start noticing the differences between insiders and noninsiders. They become more pragmatic and spend less time worrying about the apparent inconsistencies between their actions and the written procedures. They may complain about the ineffectiveness of the rules, but they decide to observe the methods of the insiders and find ways to get things done—despite the rules.

Written Versus Unwritten Rules

A *written rule* generally covers the usual, customary routine situation and the standard procedures. For example, Fred's written job description includes his handling of all mail going between the third floor and the mailroom. Most of the time, that's just fine. However, insiders on the third floor also know the *unwritten rules* for exceptional situations concerning the mail. They know not to have Fred take things to the mailroom when it's crucial that they go out on time. Fred has a tendency to get waylaid at Helen's desk on the way to the mailroom, and things end up getting out late every once in a while. Usually, that's no problem, but when something *must* get out on time, it's better to have Kim do it. Kim doesn't mind doing this every once in a while, even though it's not in her job description, because the cafeteria is next to the mailroom. It gives her a chance to grab a bag of potato chips on the way back to her desk.

And that leads to an unwritten rule about the unwritten rule: If you ask Kim too often, she'll feel that you don't appreciate her or that you don't respect her status as a superior to Fred. Also, just as there are exceptions to the written rules, there may be exceptions to the unwritten rules: You might have heard that Kim just had a check-up, and her doctor told her to stay off salty foods—or that Helen's out sick for two weeks.

Rules and Exceptions

Two functional directors of a major division of a Fortune 500 chemical company exemplify the written-rules-only versus the insider approaches: Ray Dettmer, the director of marketing, represents the "what works" approach; Norma Fleming, the director of research and development, represents the "rule-following" approach.

> *Ray:* Norma, I hear you need a typist. Could I loan you one of my aces for a few days?
>
> *Norma:* Oh, I couldn't let you do that. That would be an accounting and payroll nightmare! No. That would never do. Still . . .

I don't know how I'm going to manage, though. I've got to get that report finished by Friday!

Ray: Listen, Norma. Whether you're dealing with companies or with people, you have to fit the rules to the situation. I know I was having a real problem until last month, when I got to give my top salesperson a 25 percent raise.

Norma: You did what? That's impossible! When I asked the general manager for a 15% raise for my top research engineer, I was told that company policy puts the ceiling at 10 percent.

Ray: That's what I'm talking about. For exceptional actions, you need exceptional justification.

Norma: What do you mean by "exceptional justification"? I documented my salary recommendation in great detail, included the reasons and numbers. It was a well-done report.

Ray: Cool down and I'll explain. Six months ago, I figured out that my top salesperson was unhappy about the level of her compensation and that I needed to do something about it before her attitudes affected her performance. I felt that we might even lose her to a competitor, which would be very expensive to the company. For one thing, I've invested a lot of my time and energy developing her potential. And, since she came here, she has learned a lot of inside information about the company, not to mention an impressive list of customers that are her personal accounts. If she left, a lot of her customers would probably follow her or at least be lost to our company. If we don't sell today, the entire operation grinds to a halt tomorrow. So I came up with a plan to justify a raise of 15 percent more than the corporate guideline in this case. I launched a coordinated campaign to prime the general manager six months before I intended to make the request. I really networked it; I asked people in key positions to make positive comments about my candidate. I called on my subordinates, some of my peers, and some of my contacts for their help. Of course, I took every opportunity to let the general manager know that my super salesperson deserved an exceptional salary increase.

Norma: That's not fair! You're showing favoritism! I treat all my people alike. Rules are rules. You're supposed to follow them. Without rules, we'd have chaos.

Ray: We do have rules, rules, and more rules—for the usual situations. But, we can't possibly write enough rules for every possible contingency. In exceptional situations, people have to find exceptional solutions. Sometimes, we have to go beyond the rules.

Like Norma and Ray, technically competent managers within the same division of the same company can have very different views of their company. Just look at the differences between Norma's view and Ray's view. They disagreed about

- The nature of rules: general guidelines versus specific directives
- Uniform application versus appropriate modification of rules
- Use of rules for managing people
- Need for finding and following the unwritten rules

The Nature of Rules: General Versus Specific

Norma's View. Rules are meant to be specific directives, telling you exactly what to do and how to do it. Rules are *not* made to be broken; they should be followed exactly. If you have a situation in which the rules don't seem to tell you what to do, (1) look more thoroughly in the rules, or (2) ask someone higher up to tell you what the rules should be. Do exactly what the rules said or what your superior told you that the rules would say if they were there. One of the two big problems with rules are that there sometimes aren't enough rules and you have to find someone to tell you what to do.

Ray's View. Rules are meant to be general guidelines, telling you how to handle most of the routine, standard situations you run across. They should be followed whenever they seem to work well in the situation. However, rules should not be taken as absolute laws if they don't work well. If you have a situation in which the rules don't seem to tell you what to do, (1) see if the standard procedures can be slightly modified to fit the situation, or (2) ask a few colleagues and others in your insider network how they have handled similar situations, and look at their ideas and a few of your own ideas in order to come up with a new, unwritten rule for the situation.

Two problems with rules are that (1) sometimes the rules are too general, and you don't have enough guidelines for handling a tricky situation, and (2) sometimes the rules are too specific, and you have to change them or ignore them in order to handle a situation that the rules didn't allow for.

The Inside View. The public mask of an organization is a complex system of written and spoken rules that can apply to nearly everything, including organization charts (overt hierarchy of jobs), company rules of conduct, job descriptions and specifications, operating procedures, compensation procedures, company policies, and corporate procedures.

However, as Ray said, "we can't possibly write enough rules for every possible contingency." Nor does an organization have the time to write specifications for every single task that must be completed in order for work to be done. If employees were to work only according to the written rules and job descriptions, operation of the organization would come to a grinding halt. Many tasks are not written into anyone's formal responsibility, but these tasks must be done in order for work to flow smoothly.

Therefore, for many of the small and large nonroutine, exceptional tasks and situations, people discover or create the unwritten rules for getting things done within the organization. These rules are just as orderly and logical to follow as the written rules. However, they aren't as easy to find or to see. People in the organization must work to find this inside information.

Uniform Application Versus Appropriate Modification of Rules

Norma's View. All rules must be uniformly applied to all persons and to all situations. If you don't apply all rules to all situations, you risk getting into trouble with your supervisors. If managers don't apply the rules, they set a bad example for their people, and then their subordinates will start breaking the rules, too. Pretty soon, you end up with total chaos.

If you have a situation in which the rules don't seem to be working, complain about the situation, but continue to follow the rules. Keep hoping that eventually someone will pay attention to your complaints and will change the rules. Until then, follow the rules to the letter. The second of the two problems with rules is that sometimes you have to do something that doesn't work for a long time until the rules can be changed.

Ray's View. Some rules are necessary in order to avoid chaos. The written rules should be followed most of the time, for most of the people, in most situations. However, if you have a situation in which the rules don't seem to be working, try to modify the rules, or come up with a new guideline. If the modifications or new unwritten rules seem to work well for you, pass the information along through the insider network. Eventually, if it works well for others, think about suggesting a change of the written rules to include these exceptions.

The Inside View. Even if all tasks that are needed now were described, new tasks would have to be described tomorrow, when the consumer market, the supplies, the equipment, the personnel, or the procedures changed. Also, unanticipated exceptions constantly arise. These exceptions quickly pile up and disrupt the work flow.

However, though these unwritten rules are constantly changing, they are still orderly guidelines for getting things done in the organization. The insiders in the organization carefully follow the unwritten rules when handling exceptional situations.

However, breaking the written rules, and following the unwritten rules, does involve taking a risk. If the hidden strategies don't work, you could be in trouble for both not succeeding and not following the rules. However, because you've consulted others, you're more likely to succeed. And if you do succeed, you now have an additional unwritten rule or hidden strategy that has been tried and found to work.

Using Rules for Managing People

Norma's View. All rules must be applied equally to all persons and to all situations. If you don't apply all rules to all people, you're unfair. Managers who break the rules are going to have problems because people will know they're using favoritism. People's feelings get hurt, and you stir up a lot of bad feelings if you don't treat everyone exactly the same.

Ray's View. All rules should be applied equitably, with everyone having an equal opportunity to contribute to and to benefit from the organization. However, people who contribute exceptionally to the organization should benefit exceptionally from it. Also, *equity* is not the same as *equality.*

For example, Kareem has always put in lots of extra hours on the job. I have never doubted that he puts in far more than his share of time on the job. Last month, Kareem's wife left him with the full responsibility for their three young children. His mother was helping him with the child care, but she had to get to her own job at 4:00 pm. So he asked if he could start two hours earlier and leave two hours earlier. I decided to allow him to work on a different schedule than the other employees. His work schedule is not *equal* to everyone else's, but it is *equitable.*

Since then, I've asked each person in the department what they thought of Kareem's work schedule. Everyone seems to think it's working out well because they've seen how hard he works. I had been afraid that others might want to change their schedules, too, but no one else wants to be at work by 6:00 am! And Kareem still puts in long hours because he starts long before anyone else. He says he can get a lot done when it's quiet around here. It's worked out well for everyone.

The Inside View. Management is the process of getting things done through other people. Managers differ regarding how to accomplish this objective. The written rules prescribe certain ways of handling *superiors* (people on a higher level in the organizational hierarchy), *peers* (people on the same level), and *subordinates* (people on a lower level). But the written rules don't provide any guidance for responding to people according to the subtle differences among them. Nor do the written rules offer suggestions for handling unusual situations or special circumstances. For managing people effectively, managers must know the inside information revealed in the unwritten rules of the organization.

Need for Finding and Following the Unwritten Rules

Norma's View. The what?

Ray's View. I definitely could not get half as much accomplished if I didn't know about the unwritten rules that tell what really goes on around here. If you have any intention of going anywhere in your career, start looking for the unwritten rules of your organization. And I'm showing most of my subordinates how to follow them, too. I want them to be ready to replace me when I'm promoted to my next job.

The Inside View. Participants in organizations must invent new ways of getting work done. New problems require new solutions, but documentation lags behind. Therefore, if something legitimately needs to be done, and the organization has not formally invented a way to do it (public mask), someone will invent a way to get it done (hidden face). Somehow, those things that must be accomplished will be done. When a public-mask procedure is too inefficient or cumbersome, it is likely to be replaced by a hidden-face process.

One set of processes almost never described by written procedures is the development of working relationships between you and your boss and between you and your co-workers. Although these relationships make up the understructure of your work group, they are considered far too complex to write procedures about. These processes are so critical that they can produce the two extremes of management capability. At one extreme, they can produce a high-potential team with exceptionally effective working relationships between you, your boss, and your co-workers. At the other extreme, they can produce a work group with exceptionally ineffective relationships in which teamwork is two four-letter words.

Beginning a New Job

How to Search for the Unwritten Rules

On your first day on a new job, you confront the tasks of becoming familiar with both your organization and your new job situation within it. Your organization includes the entire set of jobs, the people on them, and their working environments. Your job situation includes only (1) your job and the jobs of those you work with and around, (2) the people with whom you work, and (3) your physical working environment.

Most organizations will introduce you to some of your co-workers and describe your organization and your job situation in general terms. Initially, most of the information will be about the public mask. You may be given lots of written material describing the public mask. Read it, but don't stop there. Remember that this public-mask information is useful for describing your organization to outsiders. Your task is to uncover the hidden face so that you can become an effective insider.

You begin your search for the hidden face the first day on the job by communicating your inquiring attitude to your boss and your co-workers. Let them know that you intend to learn and grow professionally on the job. They know more about your job situation and your organization than you do, and you hope that some of them will share what they have learned. In exchange, you will repay this kindness by helping them in the future.

Search Actively. Your attitude should be one of actively seeking understanding rather than passively waiting to be told. People enjoy talking about their jobs to interested and appreciative listeners. Show your interest by *actively listening*: Nod your head affirmatively, and verbalize your understanding in several ways ("I see." "Uh-huh." "Hmmm." "Right.").

In addition, when the information seems significant, confirm that you understand it by paraphrasing back what has been said to you. For example, suppose that your co-worker has said, "Both Tonio and Francis have keys to the supply cabinet, but be sure to ask Francis for your supplies. If you ask Tonio, he'll give you the Inquisition about what you're going to do with them." You might respond by saying, "I'll be sure to ask Francis when I need supplies. I don't want to be grilled just because I need a new pen." This tells your co-worker that you were really listening and understood the message. An extra benefit of active listening is that if you didn't fully understand the message, the speaker can tell you again in a way that you will understand. Thus, you avoid learning misinformation.

A second aspect of active listening is to ask appropriate and probing questions. Often, your questions simply seek more information
and communicate interest ("How did that happen?" "What did you
do *then*?"). Sometimes, however, you must ask questions because
you didn't understand what was said. Don't hesitate to ask these
kinds of questions. It's far better to ask a second time than to remain
forever ignorant or misinformed. Sometimes, in fact, admitting that
you don't understand something is a good way to ask for added
information that might hint at some of the unwritten rules not nor-
mally shared with newcomers. When you're new on a job is the
time you can most easily get away with asking "dumb" questions.
Use this time wisely.

Admitting ignorance is difficult for many people. We fear that
people will see us as less capable. However, many competent managers see this as a valued skill. They learn how to admit their ignorance without appearing incompetent. They accomplish this by
admitting their ignorance in the preface to their conversation and
follow this admission with comments and questions that reveal a
good deal of understanding. Of course, this skill requires confidence
to take a risk, and it improves with practice. However, it can be a
powerful instrument to communicate that you do not have all of the
answers and that you are seeking a better understanding.

Don't Push Too Hard. Although many of your co-workers like to
talk about their job situation at appropriate times, few of them enjoy
being interrogated or quizzed. Your questions should evolve naturally from the situation and flow in an informal conversation. Early
warm-up questions should be easy to answer and nonthreatening,
while later questions may become progressively more probing.

Over time, the quality of information exchanged between co-workers improves with the quality of the working relationship. Just as
you must patiently work to develop some of your most valued working relationships, so too you must gradually build some of your best
sources of information.

It takes time to understand inside information. Invest the necessary time, and persist as pieces of information gradually fall into
place. Not everyone will understand how various insider processes
work, but many will have some key information. Your task is to
gather this information from various people and to assemble it into

Exercise. Active Listening

At first, active listening may seem awkward. Ask a partner (your spouse, friend, lover, roommate) to practice this technique with you, using some of the following topics. Take turns being the one to speak and the one to actively listen. After a few sessions, active listening will feel more natural. Incidentally, it may improve your personal relationship as well. Possible topics:

• A work-related problem
• A personal problem not related to your partner
• Personal hopes and fears and aspirations for your career

Try not to let the talking move away from what the speaker wants to tell you. Really show that you're interested in what your partner is saying. After you've practiced just listening to what your partner is saying, take turns telling one another how to do something you don't already know how to do (e.g., how to repair something, how to cook something, or how to play a game). Then try either doing it yourself (with your partner's supervision) or telling your partner how to do it. This should be a good test of your active listening skills.

a working understanding. Next, we turn to some issues that complicate this task.

Don't be Fooled. Be careful not to give the impression that you can be easily misled by false information. Occasionally, some co-workers may give you false or misleading information. This may be because the person who gives it also misunderstands it or because the person communicates ineffectively. (Active listening helps you minimize problems from miscommunication.) And on rare occasions, some co-workers may even intentionally misinform, whether to tease you, to test you, or to beat you as a competitor.

In any case, do not naively accept all information as valid; test it before you act on it. If a co-worker does fool you once with false information, determine not to repeat this mistake. Find alternative sources of information, and continually test the information you obtain from this person.

Co-workers who give false information earn a reputation for dishonesty and untrustworthiness. And those co-workers who help new employees also gain a reputation—for trustworthiness and cooperation. Carefully assess your co-workers as sources of information: Test information derived from one person by asking a second and a third person. By talking to a number of different co-workers about the same issues and events and comparing agreement and disagreement, you can begin to sort out the credible from the non-credible sources on various topics.

A side benefit of this procedure is that once your co-workers know that you are checking their information with others, they will become less likely to give you false information. Few people enjoy having co-workers doubt their truthfulness.

How to Discover the Inside of Your Organization

Now that you know how to find credible sources of information, you are ready to search for the hidden face of your organization. This book describes a large number of features of the hidden faces of various organizations. These features should be taken as plausible features of your organization, and you can investigate them when they're relevant. Some of these features will be found in almost all organizations while others will be more rare.

Organizations of all kinds have both a public mask and a hidden face. Even small offices show differences between how things should be done (public mask) and how things actually are done (hidden face). Sometimes these differences are trivial, but often they are critical to effective functioning. Knowing about these differences and their implications in other organizations permits you to identify similar differences in your company. When you understand how a given process really works (hidden face), you are more likely to be effective in making it work. Even where precise procedures are specified, they may not be adequate.

Black Magic Case

Maruka Josefowicz, the director of quality control for a major industrial ink manufacturer, describes the critical procedures of her function as "black magic." When a batch of ink mixed according to the standard recipe fails to meet specifications, her people are called on to fix it. Because of the complex chemical structures of the raw materials, catalysts often result in unintended consequences. Once such a consequence occurs, bringing the batch back into specifications requires educated trial and error. If her black magic fails, the batch becomes either low in value—or worse, waste. Maruka has a difficult time, however, in convincing incoming college graduates that they should try to fix the imperfect batch instead of throwing it out and starting over again. In school, the aspiring chemists were carefully trained to discard anything that wasn't done perfectly the first time. In the real world of costly supplies, however, this practice could decimate a budget. These chemist practitioners must learn the unwritten rule that when something can be fixed instead of discarded, they should do so. They'll save money for their organization, and they'll save their jobs in the process. Unfortunately, Maruka finds that she can't afford to keep employees who don't grasp this unwritten rule.

Find the Right Questions. You begin the process of unmasking the hidden face by searching for the right questions to ask. This activity is critical. You and your informants have limited time to devote to this task. Some time and effort must be invested in finding the critical issues that make a difference between your being effective and being ineffective on the job. Questions that don't make that difference should be left aside until you have answered the critical questions.

The first step in finding the right questions involves generating a list of alternative questions about your job situation. Buy an attractive notebook that fits into your pocket, your briefcase, or your desk drawer. Immediately open it, and start writing questions you now have about your job. Each day, add comments, answers, suggestions, and more questions to your journal.

In this way, you decrease the chances that you will exhaust your energy and the patience of your informants while answering the wrong questions. Next, we turn to the process of finding answers to your right questions.

Exercise.

Question the assumptions that you have made about your job. For example, in Chapter 1, you saw that your job description does not accurately reflect all your unwritten job responsibilities. Think about when the description was written and when it was last updated. Has the job changed since the last update? Note all the areas in which your description of your job differs from the written description of it.

Another common false assumption is that your job description is a contract that, when fulfilled, will lead to a positive performance evaluation. To counter this inaccurate presumption, you must ask still more questions: What are the critical responsibilities and duties of my job? What must be done first? What must be given the most attention? What will make the most difference on my performance evaluation? What will contribute most to my career progress?

These questions about priorities often become very complex. You cannot do everything at once, but frequently, several conflicting activities compete for your immediate attention. How do you decide? There may be a standard set of priorities, but when exceptional events occur, the priorities may need to be changed. A working understanding of how the system is working helps in making these tough decisions.

Once you have assembled a list of potential right questions, test each alternative by asking whether the answer to it would make a difference in your work performance between being effective and being ineffective. Those questions that are likely to make the most difference are the ones that you need to answer first. Those next most likely should be answered second, and so on. In other words, you need to construct a list of concerns, with the most critical questions at the top and the least critical at the bottom. You start at the top and work your way down.

Find the Answers to Your Questions. Every job, every person, and every procedure has a story. Stories may reveal features of the hidden face that cannot be communicated in more direct form. Become an active student of your job situation and of your organization. You can do this by asking your right questions about how things really work, seeking and listening to stories, observing events, and looking for explanations. You may begin by searching for the history of your job situation and your organization. How did it originate, and how has it evolved? What are its success stories? Its failure stories?

Refine your questions over time as you understand more about the subject. Unmasking the hidden face in a particular area is like peeling back leaves of lettuce—one leaf at a time until you get to the heart of it. Answers to one set of inquiries leads to a refined set of questions. Over time, both questions and answers improve, partly as a function of better understanding, but also as a function of becoming a more trusted listener. Your co-workers will hesitate to talk to acquaintances about areas where the hidden face and the public mask of your organization make very different prescriptions. These matters are only discussed with people they trust and often only on a need-to-know basis. Therefore, you need to convince them that you can be trusted and need to know.

It should be clear that the learning process is one of finding problems (What are the right questions to answer?), seeking solutions (How can I get the right answers to these questions?), and implementing solutions (How can I make the right answer work?). This three-phase process is discussed more fully in Chapter 7, though no standard list of right questions can be provided to cover all situations in all organizations. Instead, you will learn how to generate your own list, with the help of the information in this book.

Discover the Multiple Realities Within Your Organization. You will find that different people will focus on different parts of the story, and you will be given several different versions of a story by different people. These different versions of a story, called "multiple realities," complicate your attempt to unmask the hidden face. *Multiple realities* come about because different people in the organization interpret the same event in very different ways. They interpret an event using their own assumptions about the hidden face. People filter all of their information through these assumptions, and they assign meanings to events based on these assumptions. This filtering process is understandable because each person only views events from one perspective—from a particular position within the organization.

Different functional groups, such as sales, operations, engineering, accounting, and human resources tend to interpret organizational events using their own filters. Typically, these filters reflect the group's hopes and fears regarding their common interests. It's crucial for you to know the different kinds of filters used by each functional group. Once you identify these filters, you can use them to understand how various groups are likely to interpret and react to various events. If you can only see your own perspective, you will be unable to understand and predict how others will react to a situation. If, on the other hand, you can grasp multiple realities, you can see more clearly how things are likely to work in your organization.

In one small (400 employees) plant of a Fortune 500 company in the automotive industry, my team and I interviewed employees from various departments about a problem perceived by plant management. The problem was that production foremen were granting permission to shop floor people to do things that were prohibited by the collective bargaining contract. Once permission was granted in a special case, legal precedent was established for the general case. Foremen were giving away management prerogatives.

Each functional group in the plant interpreted this problem differently. Each focused on a different piece of the puzzle. Plant management saw the problem as one of training the foremen in proper contract administration. Foremen viewed it as a problem of motivating workers to do their jobs effectively. Shop-floor workers interpreted it as a problem in the relationship between plant management and foremen. And officers in a local union attributed the problem to inadequate motivation of foremen. Note that none of the functional groups accepted responsibility for this problem in their interpretations of the situation.

After investigating these multiple realities, our own in-

terpretation combined all of these perspectives. In synthe-
sizing these views, we came up with a problem no one else
had considered: inadequate decision-making authority.
Foremen were not given adequate decision-making authority by plant management to both effectively motivate
their shop-floor workers and competently administer the
contract, and the foremen were frustrated by this state of
affairs.

Once we found the root problem, management and foremen were able to work out a solution that both motivated
the workers and preserved the integrity of the contract.

A useful practice is to entertain several different versions of reality
for later testing. Each version can be tested on the job over time. If
one version doesn't appear to fit your experience, don't discard it,
but file it away. It may prove useful in the future.

How to Unmask Your Job Situation

Focus on Your Own Unit. Though you should recognize and understand multiple realities within your organization, you need not
understand every aspect of your organization and its constituents
when you first begin your job. Much of this larger environment has
little immediate impact on your job. You should focus your attention
on the processes, people, and structures on which you depend to
get your work done or those in which others depend on you to get
their work done.

Initially, focus on only the people with whom and around whom
you work on a daily or weekly basis. Start with your boss and your
immediate co-workers, and get to know them and what they do.
Include your job and the jobs immediately related to yours. Start
with the situations that arise within this narrow focus and try to
understand them in terms of both the public mask and the hidden
face. Do not enlarge your focus, except as needed to deal with special
problems, until you have a working understanding of your immediate job situation.

After you have a working understanding of your immediate job
situation, you can enlarge your focus selectively to include your
entire unit and units related to it. In other words, the task of un-

masking the hidden face does not require a tremendous investment of time and energy when you know what, where, and how to search.

As you are promoted or transferred to other positions, you simply repeat the process of unmasking the hidden face in the new locale. As you move around and up the hierarchy of the organization, you become knowledgeable about many different parts. This knowledge can serve you well in terms of your effectiveness and your career progress.

Learn About Your Job. Start to develop a working understanding of your job situation by focusing on your job. Your job involves three basic features:

1. *Duties* (things you do) that you agree to perform
2. *Responsibilities* (functions you accept) that you agree to fulfill
3. *Authorities* (empowerments to do things) that enable you to perform your duties and fulfill your responsibilities

Public-mask descriptions of these job elements can be precise and exhaustive (specific), or they can be vague and incomplete (general). In any case, treat these descriptions as a starting point, not as a final description of your job possibilities. For one thing, you need to find out what you need to learn and then develop the opportunity to learn it. Starting with your job description, find new directions in which to grow.

Your job could be an opportunity for growth, or it could be a dead end. Ultimately, you must decide which it will become. Find out how others have grown out of their jobs in your job situation. If no one has, find out what keeps people back. You may be the first in your job situation to do it. If someone has grown out of your job, talk to that person about how it was accomplished.

If you truly see no opportunities within this organization or this department once you outgrow it, start thinking about where the opportunities do exist, as well as how you can get there. Make sure, however, that you learn all you can from this job in order to outgrow it before you leave. Also, use this job as a resource for building good working relationships that may provide links to your next job. Try not to burn bridges behind you; instead, maintain added bonds in your network of supportive relationships.

Learn About Your Boss. If you intend to use your job as a platform from which to launch your career rather than a prison in which you serve your time, you need the support of your boss. Very few people outgrow their jobs without the active support of their immediate superior. Your immediate superior is the most critical other person in your job situation. Find out if any of your superior's immediate subordinates have grown out of their jobs. If your superior has promoted others, you should be able to do the same. If not, you will have some selling to do. This may also be a danger sign that you must seek a broader network within the organization. You may even have to think about looking for a different job—still remembering to build bridges and to learn before you leave.

Develop a working understanding of your boss and your boss's job. What does your boss want from his or her career? What does your boss expect from the staff? How can your boss be influenced to support your career growth? How can you help your boss be more effective? These are but a few of the questions that you need to answer.

Learn About Your Co-workers. Effectiveness in organizations requires teamwork. You need to develop a working understanding of the people with whom you work, as well as of the jobs they do. Your co-workers can enhance your effectiveness, and you can enhance theirs. Your goal is to make those around you want you to succeed. Some co-workers already know how to get things done in spite of the established system. These special people tend to be linked to other competent people who also do things that seem impossible. In Chapter 1, Secret 8, I called these networks of co-workers "competence networks." These networks are not visible on the organization's written documents, but they can be found in the inside information if you know how to look. In Chapter 6, I describe more fully how you can identify and join competence networks.

Learn About Your Job Environment. Your job environment includes those parts of the organization that have an impact on your job. Poor quality work by those either upstream or downstream of your work can reflect on your effectiveness. For example, if you are in a sales position, those people who service your accounts can affect your effectiveness with your clients. Repeat sales for you are more difficult when service by others is of low quality.

People in interrelated units can make a difference to your effectiveness, and you should study them. Finding the competence network in such units is essential to your effectiveness. In fact, avoid sharing your problem with just whoever answers the phone in another unit. That person may make your problems worse. Instead, share your problems with only those people in whom you have confidence. You can develop confidence in people by taking the time to get to know them and their work. In this way, while you are developing confidence in them, they are coming to trust you.

Anticipate Consequences of Your Actions. Look at possible consequences before you leap into using your secret knowledge of your job and your organization in order to make something happen. Think about what you plan to do in terms of potential positive and negative consequences of your actions. For example, when you use the hidden strategies for succeeding in your job, you alert others that you are aware of the unwritten rules and hidden strategies. This may cause competitors to be more wary of you. Or it may increase your boss's or your co-workers' expectations of you to such a degree that you find it more difficult to obtain the information, time, or resources you need in order to succeed in your job. Avoid impulsively using the hidden strategies and secrets of your organization. Instead, think carefully about the ways in which your planned actions could go wrong, and plan for ways in which you might handle the negative consequences.

Summary

Ray Dettmer and Norma Fleming demonstrated how two managers can differ on fundamental conceptions about their company. They had different views about the nature of company rules, the proper application of rules, the task of managing people, and the career progress of subordinates.

Reading the unwritten rules of your organization requires that you be aware that the public mask does not contain all of the information that you need to be effective on your job. Companies also have hidden faces that can be revealed through active, positive, skeptical inquiry. You can start the first day on the job and continue until you have a working understanding of your job situation and your company. Some ways of finding the right questions, the right sources of information, and the right interpretations were discussed.

Reading the unwritten rules is important because it can make the difference between the fast track and the slow track for you and between effectiveness and ineffectiveness for both you and your organization.

3

Find Out Whether You're on the Fast Track Now

Bad things can happen to the careers of good people who neglect to take charge of their own careers, thereby leaving it to others to determine how fast and how high they will rise in their organizations. Your career is too important to you to entrust it into the hands of others. Your first step in managing your own career is to find out whether you're on the fast track right now. Most organizations don't make it easy to discover who is or isn't on the fast track. But you can find out. This chapter will help you discover the hidden strategies used by supervisors with their fast-track subordinates. Once you know whether you're already on the fast track, you can steer the course of your own career more knowledgeably.

Training Is the Minimum Requirement

In their first four months on the job in a high-turnover service industry, not all new clerical employees were trained to do their jobs. Supervisors quickly decided to train some of them and not to train others. Actually, the supervisors imposed a self-fulfilling prophecy on the new employees. They thought they knew which new employees would stay and which would leave, and they acted on this belief. They spent a minimum of time and energy on the ones they thought would leave.

In contrast, they spent a lot of time and energy helping the ones they predicted would stay. Supervisors would spend extra time coaching and getting to know those whom they expected to stay. Moreover, they asked for and patiently answered these employees' job-related questions.

However, those who were predicted to leave were advised to find the answers to their job questions without bothering them. In fact, they were frequently referred to a manual to find answers to their questions. Not surprisingly, by the end of 12 weeks, most of the "short-timers" did, in fact, leave. This further reinforced the supervisors' confidence in their own judgment and determination to follow this practice again with other new employees.

What are some of the early signals of disaster, and what should be done about them? New employees in high-turnover situations may find that their supervisors develop a self-fulfilling prophecy and act on it.

New employees require some training to learn the basics of their jobs; however, if you are not getting even the minimum, you should act quickly. Talk to your co-workers about how to get your supervisor to give you more direction. Check out possible self-fulfilling prophecies to determine whether you are seen as likely to be a short-timer. Armed with this information, talk to your supervisor about your long-term aspirations with the company and how you want to earn your way.

If your supervisor doesn't begin to increase the amount of time spent on training you, after your repeated attempts to convince your boss that you are an exception to the self-fulfilling prophecy, more drastic measures are called for. Within the job, start building collaborative working relationships with your co-workers. Solicit information from them in the beginning. As you learn more, give them whatever information you've gleaned. Continue to learn as much as possible from this job while building work contacts that may permit you to find and move to a more supportive environment.

Most work situations, however, aren't this barren of support. Most supervisors gladly help you to master your present job because it is their job (even in the written rules) to help you do your job effectively. The better you work, the better they look. However, being effectively trained to do your present job is *not* enough to get you on the fast track.

"No One Told Me I Wasn't on the Fast Track"

Following the Written Rules. Broderick MacNeil worked as an accountant in one of the large technical divisions of a leading multinational Fortune 500 corporation, based in the United States. He had always been an above-average student in school and had graduated from college with honors. A semester before graduation, he had looked over several organizations and decided that this corporation offered him the greatest opportunities for advancement.

On the job, Broderick had always completed his work efficiently, thoroughly, accurately, and in a timely manner, working overtime (unpaid) as needed. Whenever his boss asked him to do anything extra, he always gladly cooperated and completed the assignment exactly as requested. He worked diligently, patiently expecting that he would be rewarded with promotions when the time was right. Broderick followed the written rules exceptionally well.

Revealing a Corporate Secret. In 1988, Broderick's division implemented a rigorous performance evaluation program. Once the evaluations were completed, the evaluators did something extremely unusual: They told the employees how they viewed the employees' relative potential for promotion. Within each job level below the directors of the company, employees were classified into four groups, based on their promotion potential. The highest performers were called "fast-trackers," and the lowest performers were called "slow-trackers." The other two categories of performance were either slightly above or slightly below average.

The managers of the performance evaluation program had expected that this rare display of corporate honesty would have beneficial effects on managers and technicians. They expected above-average and superior performers to be motivated by this recognition of their excellence. And they expected below-average and inferior performers to be motivated by this attention to their need to improve. They did not, however, specify exactly how these benefits would occur. The actual consequences of this candor astounded the program's managers.

Reacting to the Disclosure. Broderick was told that he was "above average," but that he was not a "fast-tracker." He felt hurt: "What have I done wrong? I always thought I was doing fine. I haven't made any major goofs, and I always accept extra work when I'm asked to." He felt outraged: "Why wasn't I told this sooner? Haven't I done everything I was told to do? Why didn't anyone tell me I wasn't on the fast track?" He felt disappointed and confused: "Now what should I do? If I don't know what I did wrong, how can I do it right? Do I have to start all over, proving myself?" And he was puzzled: "How do I get to the fast track? What should I do differently?"

Broderick certainly wasn't the only one to react negatively to the revelations. Though Broderick was disappointed, those employees who were told that they were slow-trackers or below average were shocked. Though Broderick felt hurt, they were devastated. They had previously never realized that their careers had reached dead ends with this company. They felt cheated that no one had ever even hinted to them that they were on the slow track. "Why weren't we told earlier that we needed to improve?"

Perhaps most surprising to the program managers, even the fast-trackers didn't enthusiastically welcome the evaluations. Marie Fournier, a fast-tracker in Broderick's unit, said, "I enjoyed getting the official word that I'm on the right track, but I had already felt pretty sure of where I stood. My boss has been letting me know my worth at least once a week. And I hated seeing what it did to everyone else. Team morale plummeted, and it took us months to get back to being productive again. Some people still haven't recovered." Marie was not unusual among the fast-trackers: Most had already been receiving frequent affirmation of their value and signals of appreciation. Hearing that they were fast-trackers was not news to them.

Moral of the Story: Corporate Versus Personnel Perspective

The lessons to be learned from this example differ according to whether you view it from the perspective of the corporation or from the perspective of the worker.

The Corporation's View. Needless to say, it does not seem wise to reveal corporate secrets on a sudden and widespread basis. This suggests one of two strategies: (1) Keep the secrets well guarded from everyone indefinitely, or (2) gradually and selectively inform some people of some of the secrets, but don't tell them bad news if you can avoid it.

If you are a corporation using the first strategy, you make sure that no one finds out who is or isn't on the fast track. If people ask whether they're on the fast track, avidly deny that tracks exist; insist that everyone has an equal opportunity to be advanced if they follow the written rules. Make sure that all supervisors follow this policy.

If you are a corporation using the second strategy, selectively tell fast-trackers, almost-fast-trackers, almost-slow-trackers, and slow-trackers different things. At a discreet time and place, tell the fast-trackers that they are on the fast track; invest time and resources in developing their careers because this will definitely pay off later in their careers. As early in their careers as possible, tell the almost-fast-trackers how to get to the fast track, and invest some time and resources in their career development; it will probably pay off later.

Tell the almost-slow-trackers and slow-trackers nothing if they perform their jobs adequately; invest as little as possible in their careers, as you will get little return on your investment. Give them cost-of-living increases and occasional adjustments in their job titles to reflect their years of experience. If they don't perform their jobs adequately, or if the needs of the corporation change, phase them out, lay them off, or fire them—with or without a warning to improve.

The Worker's View. If you're an employee, your view is very different indeed! Your goal is to find out as many of the secrets as you can as early as possible in your career. If you work for a first-strategy corporation, this will be more difficult than if you work for a second-strategy one. But don't be deceived by denials that promotion-linked evaluations exist.

If you can't get a straight answer from your supervisor, you can still figure this out for yourself. Notice that the corporation using the second strategy invests in employees differently, according to whether they're *on* the fast track, *close* to it, or way *off*. Corporations that deny having a fast track do this, too. These differences in corporate investments are your clues as to whether you're on or close to the fast track. This chapter gives you specific insight into which investments lead to the fast track. With this insight, you can discover how you are being evaluated, in order to use that information to take charge of and manage effectively your own career.

Training Versus Investment

Note that corporations did not say, "Invest nothing in the slow-trackers and almost-slow-trackers." That would be completely unrealistic because all employees require at least some training in order to do their jobs. There are key differences, however, between training and investment.

Training enables workers to do their present job efficiently; an organization provides training in order to improve the worker's performance of the *present job*. To get a good return value for providing training, the worker should *stay* in the present job, performing it efficiently for the organization as long as possible. Thus, once the training has been completed, organizations expect the workers they train to remain with them in the jobs for which they were trained.

Investment, however, helps workers to move beyond their present jobs and to develop their *future careers* within the organization. Therefore, to get a good return value for an investment, the worker should *outgrow* the present job, staying in it only as long as is needed to learn all that can be learned within that job. Once training for the present job has been completed, the investment process begins, and organizations expect the workers they invest in to continue to grow into and out of increasingly responsible positions within the organization.

Clearly, you will need both training and investment if you are to move along the fast track in your organization. Your task is (1) to recognize those actions that indicate an investment, beyond simple training, and (2) to take advantage of the investment and offer a good return on the investment as soon as possible. If you either don't recognize the investments or don't take advantage of them, your supervisor may start to feel that the investments won't pay off. Don't let this happen!

Distinguishing Training from Investment

How can you tell when your boss is investing in your career? This may be more difficult than you expect, because at first the differences between routine training and investing can be subtle. When your boss gives you a special assignment, does it indicate training or investment? If you guess wrong, you may embarrass yourself and your boss. What can you do to increase your confidence in your judgment?

My research partners and I asked bosses what actions they took when they were *investing* in a subordinate, as opposed to what they did when they were *training* one of them. We hoped that they would agree that certain actions were used more often for investing and others for training. Fortunately, they did. Given a list of more than 20 possible supervisory actions, they agreed that the top 10 actions were used more frequently for investing and the bottom 10 actions were used more for training.

We then took our study one step further. We looked at which subordinates were actually selected for promotion and which ones weren't. We found that the only difference between the subordinates who were selected for promotion and those who were not selected was the boss's decision to invest in them via these 10 career-enhancing activities. These differences could not be attributed to differences in gender, race, or education of the subordinates. Thus, the top 10 investment actions determined whether certain selected subordinates were promoted out of their jobs or they remained in their present jobs.

Investment: The Top 10 Career-Enhancing Actions

When bosses decide to invest in the careers of selected subordinates, they must do so wisely. Such investments cost the bosses dearly in terms of their most valuable resources: their time and their energy. If they squander these resources imprudently, they will have less to devote to (a) doing their own jobs effectively, (b) outgrowing their own jobs (making room for others), and (c) investing in the careers of other subordinates (grooming their replacements). Thus, bosses generally invest in the future careers of only one or two of their subordinates. The others receive advice on how to do their present jobs effectively, but not on how to outgrow their jobs.

Table 3.1 shows the stark differences in the percentages of bosses who used these actions for their selected, as opposed to their unselected subordinates within the same units. These 10 actions clearly reflect how bosses use the investment process to promote the careers of certain selected subordinates. Though they may engage in a few of these 10 activities with unselected subordinates, they do many more of these activities more frequently with the subordinates selected for the fast track. These differences come into even sharper focus when we add that the selected and the unselected employees were the top two employees in the unit in terms of likelihood for promotion. Thus, the differences underscore the links between investments and actual promotion.

Use this information to determine whether your boss is investing in your future career or just training you in your present job. If your boss frequently engages in the following top 10 actions with you, especially if done more with you than with others in your unit, you should gain confidence that your boss is investing in you.

1. Inside information
2. Interdepartmental functioning
3. Challenging assignments
4. Visibility upstairs
5. Disaster preparedness

Table 3.1 *Critical Actions That Indicate a Boss's Investment*

Actions of Immediate Superior	Career Track	
	Fast	Slow
Provide special information through which the subordinate can learn how the company really operates*	75%	30%
Expose the subordinate to information regarding changes to be made*	60%	20%
Give the subordinate challenging assignments*	83%	44%
Talk about the subordinate's strengths with higher management	58%	20%
Prepare the subordinate for difficult assignments*	60%	25%
Advise the subordinate on long-range career plans	47%	12%
Delegate to the subordinate enough authority to complete important assignments*	83%	44%
Advise the subordinate on promotion opportunities	46%	14%
Confidentially advise the subordinate about career problems	45%	15%
Include the subordinate's input in decisions for which only the boss was responsible*	78%	50%

*This action was also found to be more frequently used during the first three years for persons who later rode the fast track up into the higher realms of the organization. In addition, the following actions were commonly received by fast-trackers during their first three years:
• Allow the newcomer to put some of his/her ideas into assignments
• Support the subordinate's actions through clear expectations, attention to work progress, willingness to help, and constructive guidance
• Develop a trusting relationship

  6. Long-range career planning
  7. Delegation of responsibilities
  8. Promotion notifications
  9. Advance warnings
 10. Input on decisions

1. Inside Information. Providing you with inside information enables you to better learn the organization's hidden strategies. As with most covert actions, giving out inside information is at the discretion of your boss. Such information is usually sensitive and illuminating: sensitive because it is somewhat incompatible with written policies and procedures, and illuminating in that it suggests how the organization really operates. In sum, inside information allows you to understand how things are done in the organization.

Examples of providing such inside information include

1. Alerting you to the organization's definitions of key terms, such as *effectiveness* and *quality*
2. Informing you about what really makes a difference in the organization, such as getting results or following the written rules
3. Practicing with you the organization's way of thinking so that you can see its logic
4. Describing to you how an executive-level organizational decision really was made so that you may begin to see what is valued and how decisions are reached.

2. Interdepartmental Functioning. Exposing you to various aspects of other departments' functions within the company teaches you how sister departments work together with your home department. It also helps you establish effective working relationships with key subordinates in sister departments. Seeing the hidden view of interdepartmental operations complements your understanding of the hidden view of the organization's operations discussed in Activity 1. In addition, developing effective working relationships across departments is essential for building your career networks. Without such networks, your career may be prematurely truncated.

Examples of such exposure include

1. Assigning you as a liaison with another department on a special program or project
2. Placing you on an interdepartmental task force or committee
3. Lending you to another department for a special program

4. Exchanging you with subordinates in another department to promote cross-training

3. *Challenging Assignments.* In order for you to outgrow your present job, you must be given challenging tasks. For this to be most beneficial, however, your boss must carefully assess your capability and the assignment's difficulty so that you must stretch your existing skills and knowledge but you won't be stretched too thinly to succeed. The assignment must be a growth experience, yet not one in which you are likely to fail. Your boss must also provide enough resources to do the job.

Examples of challenging assignments include

1. Asking you to serve as a backup to your boss on an important committee
2. Requesting that you collaborate with your boss on a special project
3. Asking you to take on an assignment that requires you to acquire inside information or to learn new skills, such as analysis, synthesis, summary, or innovation
4. Giving you the opportunity to show leadership on a group project

4. *Visibility Upstairs.* "Visibility upstairs" is one of the most valuable payoffs you can receive from your boss. Unless you are noticed by the people at higher levels in the organization, your career may never take off. The first step is to display your strengths to your boss. The next step is to motivate your boss to talk to higher management about your strengths.

Examples of providing visibility upstairs include

1. Assigning you to activities or projects that are of interest to and will be talked about with higher management
2. Nominating you for a committee that is visible to higher management
3. Recommending that you receive advanced training that requires the approval of higher management

5. *Disaster Preparedness.* Your boss can help you avoid many career-threatening mistakes by preparing you for difficult situations while you are still in relatively safe situations. Of course, your boss is not compelled to do this for you. Many bosses feel their subordinates should learn the ropes the hard way—through trial and error. Yet a majority of the selected members' bosses felt that they should protect a subordinate from such disaster. This coaching activity does require time and energy on the part of the boss.

Examples of such preparation include

1. Briefing you on the hidden risks in various activities, such as who you should and should not depend on

2. Training you in methods of discovering and avoiding certain explosive issues, such as underlying disputes

3. Counseling you in methods of dealing with certain difficult people, such as how to confront, how to negotiate, and how to accommodate

6. *Long-range Career Planning.* If your boss advises you on long-range career plans, you will find it easier to chart a career path inside your organization. Without such advice, you may make unrealistic or vague career plans. Because bosses don't lavish advice on all subordinates—not even all talented subordinates—this is a good indicator of the boss's choice for investment. Giving advice on long-range career plans suggests that the boss is interested in more than the immediate job situation or short-term self-interest.

Examples of such advice include

1. Alerting you to common career mistakes to be avoided

2. Giving you information about realistic expectations

3. Serving as an advisor to help you prepare for the next 30 to 40 years

7. *Delegation of Responsibilities.* You show your boss your relative value when she or he really needs your help. If your boss gets the needed help, your stock goes up. If not, your stock goes down. If possible, you must not only fulfill any important responsibilities the boss has delegated, but also excel in fulfilling them.

This action has the clearest payback to a boss. The previous actions directly benefit you at the expense of your boss. This one directly benefits your boss, who enjoys the extended time and energy provided by you. Of course, you also benefit from the opportunity to perform higher-level activities—a part of the boss's job.

Examples of such assignments include

1. Serving as backup to the boss on important committees
2. Collaborating with the boss on special projects and programs
3. Performing preliminary analyses for the boss to condense and focus information

8. Promotion Notifications. If your boss advises you of promotion opportunities, you are being groomed for the next career step. Whether to accept or decline a promotion is a difficult decision; seek the advice of a trusted superior.

Examples of such advice include

1. Alerting you to the full array of promotional paths
2. Briefing you on various risks and mistakes in promotion decisions
3. Notifying you of specific promotion opportunities that may be coming available in other departments
4. Counseling you about the promotional process and the next steps

9. Advance Warnings. Confidential advice about how to handle potential or existing career problems is clearly insider information, revealing an aspect of the hidden face of the organization. The level of trust and commitment demanded by this role is beyond that prescribed by the written rules. Bosses are not required to get involved in the personal problems of a subordinate, and many simply refer the subordinate to the personnel department for assistance.

Examples of this role include

1. Serving as a sounding board for your career problems
2. Suggesting courses of action to deal with your career problems
3. Actively attempting to help you solve your career problems

10. Input on Decisions. Another key sign of investment is your boss's request for input on a decision for which only your boss is responsible. By asking for your input, your boss is suggesting that you have something to contribute. Your boss values your ideas and your insight.

Examples of such participation include

1. Soliciting your ideas about a problem
2. Involving you in the decision-making process
3. Collaborating with you on solving a problem

Common Theme. Within these top 10 career-enhancing actions, note that a common thread runs among them: Most of these actions involve the bosses *sharing* parts of *their own jobs* with their subordinates. In this way, you can be groomed to outgrow your present job and demonstrate your competence in handling aspects of your boss's job. If you do this well, you make your boss look good to higher management. This means that eventually your boss may be promoted. Naturally, if you are the person who has handled your boss's job well, you are the likely candidate to replace your boss. Thus, while you help your boss to outgrow her or his job, you are outgrowing your own and growing into your boss's job.

Subordinates who are not offered these opportunities to share aspects of their bosses' jobs are not being encouraged to outgrow their present jobs. Thus, though they may have been trained well, they have not received investment activities from their bosses. Without these investments, they'll have a much harder time getting to the fast track.

If, after reading about these activities, you find that your boss is investing more in one or more of your peers than in you, Chapter 4 offers you some specific suggestions for encouraging your boss to invest in you. If you still feel unsure about the differences between investment and training, the next section shows the 10 training activities.

The 10 Training Activities

Your boss commonly uses 10 activities to train you and your peers to do your present jobs. These activities aren't an investment in your future careers. These 10 training activities don't help you to outgrow your present job. These activities generally fall within the written job descriptions of bosses. Hence, most bosses should (and do) apply the following activities equally to all subordinates:

1. Discussion of tasks. Standard, routine procedures dictate that bosses discuss with all employees the work that the subordinates are expected to accomplish within the boundaries of the employees' present jobs.

2. Discussion of effectiveness. At regular intervals, according to the normal written organizational policies, bosses are expected to meet with employees and specify the ways in which the employees can be more effective in their present jobs. These usually take the form of annual or semiannual performance appraisals, but initially, these meetings may take place much more frequently.

3. Preview of outbound documents. Part of most bosses' written job descriptions include their preview of all written reports, correspondence, and other documents prior to their transmittal out of the department (or even within the department in some cases). One reason for this to be included in the boss's role is to ensure that everything leaving the department makes the department look good. The intensity of this preview may differ among subordinates, but the frequency of it may not.

4. Guidance for presentations. Again, the reason for this to be a part of the boss's standard, routine role is to ensure that presentations show off the competence and abilities of the department, not permitting shoddy work to tarnish the department's image. The difference between selected and unselected subordinates has more to do with the content of these presentations than the degree of coaching provided for it. If the content of the presentation falls clearly within the bounds of the current job, it is likely to be training related. If it could be used as a means for outgrowing the present job, it is more likely to be an investment.

5. Specific, constructive praise. Your boss is expected to provide you with specific, constructive praise of what you do well on your current job. If, however, your boss is encouraging you to take on responsibilities that fall outside your current job description, the praise you receive may indicate that you have provided a return on your boss's investment.

6. Encouragement of innovative improvements. It is standard practice in most organizations to at least occasionally encourage innovative ways to improve the performance of employees' present jobs—particularly if the innovations work well.

7. Questioning of innovative suggestions. It is also standard practice for supervisors to question subordinates' suggestions for improvement. This "devil's advocate" role helps to ensure that the standard, written routines are generally followed, thus avoiding chaos. It also confirms whether the employee has truly thought through the consequences of the suggestion and may be a good way of testing the employee to see whether she or he merits increased investment. Individuals tend to prefer continuing with routines and practices that have been working at least adequately. The larger the organization of individuals, the greater the resistance to change. Don't interpret your boss's questioning of your suggestions as a reflection of whether your boss is investing in your future career.

8. Requests for overtime participation. Requesting that subordinates work overtime is standard practice in many organizations. Don't misinterpret such requests as reflecting a commitment to invest in your future career. If the overtime work is a part of your existing job description and the tasks you will be handling fall within your current job responsibilities, this is unlikely to reflect investment. If, on the other hand, the request for overtime involves job responsibilities that more naturally fall within the written description of your boss's job duties, this may be an investment.

9. Provision of selected inside information. To a certain extent, all jobs require possessing some degree of an organization's inside information. If your boss provides you with only the inside information you need in order to perform your current job, you are not necessarily being asked to become an insider. If, on the other hand, your boss provides you with inside information that you *don't* need in order to perform your current job, but that would help you to outgrow your current job, your boss just may be investing in you.

10. Travel to meetings or conferences. Many jobs include travel as part of their standard, written job descriptions and normal, customary routines. Being one of the many people in your department who is asked periodically to attend out-of-town meetings or conferences does not reflect investment. This is particularly true if the meeting relates directly to your present job. If, however, you are one of the few being asked to attend meetings not directly related to your present job, you may be being encouraged to outgrow the confines of your present job. In this situation, travel might be considered an investment.

Common Theme. The preceding 10 training activities rarely indicate an investment in your career. The recurring theme in these activities was that you were being helped by your boss to improve your effectiveness in performing your *present* job, not to outgrow it. The frequency (*quantity*) of these training activities probably does not indicate whether your boss wants to help you move onto the fast track.

As was suggested in a few of the activities, however, the *quality* of the activities may indicate something about whether your boss is investing in your career's future. However, differences in quality are far more subtle and difficult to determine than differences in quantity, and you may be unable to determine the quality of your boss's training activities with your peers. You may find it easier to assess the frequency of your boss's career-enhancing investment activities than to evaluate the quality of your boss's training activities.

Choice Is the Key. Not all subordinates want to take advantage of their bosses' investments. Though not everyone is offered investment, not all who are offered it accept it. You may not feel that you want to outgrow your present job. Or you may feel that you aren't ready to outgrow it yet. That's fine. The information in this chapter can still help you to recognize what you are being offered. You may even want to help the boss invest in someone else. Help your boss to pick your next boss!

In any case, if you know how to recognize the differences between investment and training, *you* are still managing your own career. If you know how to outgrow your present job but choose not to, *you* are making the choices. If, however, you don't know how to find the inside information you need, you aren't in charge of your own career; others are making your decisions for you.

Investment Payoffs for Subordinates

When Should Investment Begin?

In 1972, my colleagues and I studied all the college graduates who joined a large multinational merchandising company. We studied their company test results, their college education, their first job assignments, and their bosses' investments during their first 3 years on the job. Then we compared those factors with their career success up to 10 years later (their 13th year on the job). After looking at all the information, we found that having their bosses invest in them early in their careers predicted their later career success.

The six investment actions that are asterisked in the body of Table 3.1, and the three additional investment actions indicated in the footnote to the table were the investment actions most likely to predict future career success. If workers received these nine investment actions during the first 3 years of their careers, they were much more likely to be successful up to 10 years later.

Growing Out of Jobs Before Promotion

Career investments by the boss indicated that the person was given the opportunity to grow out of the current job and into larger responsibility and accepted it. This larger responsibility may be for a project or a product, or it may involve sharing responsibility with the superior for an entire unit. It is larger than the narrow limits of a particular job.

To fulfill this larger responsibility, the subordinate must receive information, additional authority and decision-making influence, greater attention and support from the superior, and a more effective working relationship with the superior. In addition, a subordinate obtains the career benefits of gaining both technical and managerial expertise on the job. The subordinate learns how to collaborate with someone who has superior authority and status and how to help the working relationship develop from that of strangers to that of mutually trustworthy collaborators.

In this organization, those managers who grew out of their jobs during their first 3 years of employment tended to be on the fast track 13 years later. Those who stayed within the confines of their jobs tended to remain on the slow track.

Two-Way Exchange Relationships

During the first three years, our young managers also rated their working relationships with their immediate superiors. Those receiving investments rated their bosses much higher than did their slow-track colleagues on the following items:

- Recognition of their potential
- Understanding of their problems
- Sharing of their expectations
- Willingness to collaborate
- Receptivity toward changing their job
- Support of their efforts
- Inclusion of them in social activities

Successful managers worked for superiors whom they trusted, supported, and worked hard to promote—they put the interests of their work units above those of their jobs and themselves. In exchange, their superiors trusted, supported, and worked to prepare them for promotion. Mature effective working relations are based on this kind of reciprocation. In sharp contrast, less successful managers tended not to show these characteristics. Rather, they worked for superiors who did their own jobs, and they did their jobs, and that's all either of them received from the other.

Beyond Test Scores

Results of this 13-year study showed that the bosses' investments in subordinates' careers during the first 3 years in the organization made more of a difference in their career success than did their test scores. In addition, the end of the third year, people were already on fast or slow tracks that changed very little in the following 10 years.

The career payoffs of the fast track were graphically illustrated 10 years later. Those on the fast track were in more responsible positions that paid more than those of their slower-track cohorts. They were given greater resources and more latitude to fulfill their responsibilities than those on the slower track. They more frequently developed two-way mutually collaborative relationships with their bosses, than their slower-track colleagues. Finally, they expressed greater satisfaction with their employment situation and with their working relationships than did their slower-moving cohorts. From the company's point of view, these fast-trackers were those most likely to become the future executives. They were rated as much more promotable than their slower-track colleagues. After 13 years in the company, those who were fortunate enough and/or knowledgeable enough to get their bosses to invest in their careers during their first three years were good bets to move into the executive suite. Those who didn't receive those investments during their first three years were good bets to plateau in their careers well short of the executive suite.

The Message

There are several implications of this study for your career.

Ability Isn't Everything. The fast track can be achieved by people of average ability in the best companies. In this 13-year study, neither high test scores nor attendance at a prestigious school contributed to movement onto the fast track. What did make a real difference as to who made it to the fast track were the investments made by their bosses. Those who were able to get their bosses to invest in their careers were on the right track. Getting your bosses to invest in your career is more important to your career success than your scores on entry tests.

Begin Early. Reaching the fast track is facilitated by beginning the investment process early in your career. The first month is not too soon. From the first day on the job, your boss will observe and interpret your actions. You need to send clear and consistent signals that you intend to earn investments from your bosses by promoting your bosses and outgrowing the confines of your present job. Only a few people are discovered and reach the fast track later in their careers. Such rare late bloomers generally have a rougher road to travel.

Based on the results of the 13-year study, this process of bosses' investing in some of their people began the first year in the company. Moreover, those people who received the investment the first year tended to receive it from other bosses the second and third years. Even at year 13, these same people were continuing to receive investments from their bosses and were continuing to rise on the fast track.

Earn the Help of Others. Few reach the fast track without the investments of their bosses. Without their investments, and the help of your competent co-workers, you are forced to learn the hard way and to suffer the harsh consequences. For most of us, it is far better to get others to help us by collaborating in teamwork.

Much of the important work in organizations requires teamwork through a network of competent people. Achievements by such a team are frequently much greater than those which could be achieved individually by the sum of the individuals' actions. This is not to deny the important contributions of the person working alone. But the performance of organizations that employ teamwork can far outdistance that of organizations that do not.

An Excellent Investment. Finally, the future payoffs for subordinates are well worth the effort if you enjoy improved compensation, "perks" (perquisites), and opportunities to make a real difference in your company. Career payoffs of those who receive investments from their bosses far exceed those of their slow-track cohorts.

The implications of these results are clear. Investments in your career pay off, and the sooner these investments begin, the greater your payoff. What's the payoff for your boss? Why do bosses decide to invest in their subordinates' careers?

Investment Payoffs for Bosses

Most bosses seek competitive advantages for the work units they supervise. They often attempt to increase their productive resources by negotiating larger budgets or by gaining greater support from their bosses, peers, and subordinates. They gain greater support from *their* bosses and *their* peers in the same ways you do (Chapters 4 and 6 describe these ways more fully). But gaining greater support from subordinates for other than short-term efforts usually requires a special incentive. One such incentive is to invest in the careers of those people who want to move onto a faster track. This may seem like a simple thing to do, but it can only be done at a cost: the boss's valuable time and energy.

Return on Investment

Given the enormous cost to the boss, the boss must prudently decide which of the many possible investments will be most profitable. A profitable investment from the boss's viewpoint will result in a *net gain* in time and energy within a reasonable period of time:

$$\begin{array}{c}
\text{Time and energy saved by subordinate} \\
\text{performing boss's tasks (over } x \text{ months)} \\
-\text{Time and energy invested in helping} \\
\underline{\text{subordinate outgrow job (over } x \text{ months)}} \\
= \text{Net gain (over } x \text{ months)}
\end{array}$$

Thus, a profitable investment in a person's career occurs when the person receiving the investment grows to take on enough of the boss's work that the boss realizes a net gain in available time. Thus, to be profitable, an investment must save more of a boss's time than it costs. Naturally, the greater the net gain, the better. Moreover, this net gain must be realized within a reasonable period of time. For example, if you work for a certain boss for two years, the boss would expect to break even on the investment in your career well before 18 months. Because some people take more of an investment than others to achieve the same savings in the boss's time, some people have a longer payback period than others. Bosses often consider these factors before they invest in any of their people.

At each level of the hierarchy, superiors seek to increase their available time by investing wisely in their people and using this net gain in their time to earn further investments in their own careers by *their* superiors. In this way, at each level of the organization, superiors make investments, and subordinates gain the resources and incentives to grow out of their jobs.

The Investment Decision

Bosses tend to invest in the careers of people who convince them of three things:

1. They really seek to outgrow their present jobs
2. They can complete critical assignments at acceptable levels of quality
3. They are likely to provide their boss with a net gain in available time within a reasonable period

First, you must convince your boss that you want to outgrow your job ahead of schedule, or you may be seen as a poor risk for this investment in your career: You may not be offered the opportunity for investment. When your boss is thinking about investment, you may be overlooked.

Second, you must convince your boss that you can be counted on to perform important special assignments well, or you have little chance of getting such assignments. These assignments reflect on your boss's career. To receive such an assignment, you must assure your boss that you can perform these critical assignments without demanding too much of your boss's time.

Third, as mentioned, a net gain on the investment of available time and energy must be likely within a reasonable period of time. Bosses tend not to invest in the careers of all of their subordinates. They tend to invest in only those people who meet these three criteria, and then only when they need additional resources to get the work of their units done effectively. This selective investment produces a hidden understructure within organizational units in which those who are receiving investments and giving returns on investments become trusted assistants of the boss. The other subordinates remain as hired hands. Trusted assistants take on part of their bosses work and wield some of the resources of their bosses. In return, bosses spend more time on the career development of these trusted assistants. Trusted assistants outgrow their jobs by taking on greater responsibilities and authority. Although trusted assistants enjoy the benefits and perks of employing more valuable resources and possessing greater latitude than the hired hands who stay within the confines of their job, their main payoff is the accelerated professional growth and consequent enhanced promotability.

Begin your career by becoming a trusted assistant in an entry position, then strive to become one at each level as you move up the hierarchy. This is how you can reach the fast track initially and stay on it over your entire career. Finally, trusted assistants become part of a network of competent collaborators that get things done even when others tell them that such things are impossible.

Gradualness of the Investment

Most bosses only gradually make the decision to invest in a person's career. If they are under sufficient pressure to perform, they may require additional resources from some of their people, so the bosses may offer small assignments to those whom they think (a) want to outgrow their jobs in order to be promoted, (b) are likely to complete the assignment well, and (c) will complete the assignment without creating undo demands on the boss's time.

Several things can happen after you receive an initial offer. First, you may decide to refuse the offer. You can do so legitimately by simply pointing out that you do not have enough time to do this assignment properly. This response is legitimate because this assignment falls outside of the written rules of your job, and you are not required to accept it. You are not being paid by your company to do it because it is not part of your employment agreement.

On the other hand, you may accept the offer. In this case, you expect that your boss will supply both the resources needed to do the assignment properly and the incentive to reward your decision to outgrow your job. This incentive should be the boss's investment in your career.

After you have accepted such an assignment, your performance on the assignment may yield a number of different results. For one, you may botch the assignment. This may not be the end of the process. If the boss interprets this failure as a profitable learning experience for a potentially valuable trusted assistant, such a misstep may not hurt the investment process. In contrast, if the boss views this failure as indicating a lack of drive or growth potential, this failure may signal the end of investment.

If you do well on the assignment, but you require extraordinary resources (boss's time, subordinates' time, supplies, equipment, etc.), you may still not have helped your cause. Yet your boss may appreciate your enthusiasm and perseverance in the face of great tribulation. In other words, your boss may test you with a series of initially small assignments. These assignments may grow into progressively larger assignments when such investments appear promising.

The Reinvestment Decision

Profitability of career investment can be evaluated sequentially over time, using a series of progressively more significant assignments. In this way, the complex decisions as to which people should receive the investments and how such investments should be offered can be simplified into a series of less complex decisions. Those people who reveal by their performance on early assignments that they seek to outgrow their present jobs and who make every effort to learn new skills quickly and effectively can be brought along more rapidly. Because the investment process is gradual, and the results of each step are evaluated, investment decisions become much easier for the boss. Earlier mistakes in the decision-making process can be corrected based on later information.

Both parties are involved in this learning process. Your boss learns over time what you want out of your career and what you are capable of contributing to the team. You learn over time what your boss wants and what your boss is able to contribute to your career. As the working relationship between you and your boss matures, you develop mutual trust, respect, and loyalty, and you learn the true meaning of professional teamwork. When both parties work together on building such a relationship and it succeeds, it becomes a two-way collaborative relationship that can yield the promises of the fast track for both parties.

The Three Key Signs of Investment

Thus far, we have discussed what bosses say they do when they invest in the career of one of their people, examined a 13-year study on the effects of such investment, and outlined why and how bosses invest in their people. Next, we turn to how you as a subordinate can tell when your boss is investing in your career.

In terms of the top 10 investments, three activities require investments of the boss's time and offer no direct return of the investment (i.e., they don't help the boss to save time in any way): your boss talking about your strengths with higher management, your boss advising you on promotional opportunities, and your boss serving as a confidant to you on promotional opportunities. Thus, these activities would seem to be the best indicators of investment. In fact, bosses were three times more likely to engage in these activities with selected (fast-track) subordinates than to use them with unselected subordinates. In other words, these activities do not help the boss get his work done, but they help your career development.

Many young managers also told us that they believed these three activities were the most significant. However, if their boss engaged in these three activities and did not engage in most of the remaining seven, they would not believe that they were selected for investment. Unless they were also given special information, challenging assignments, and important responsibilities, and they were brought in on some of the boss's decisions, they would have cause to be skeptical. In fact, they would wonder whether the boss was sincere in offering career advice.

What is clear is that the top 10 career-enhancing activities tend to be used together. People selected for investment by their bosses receive more of all 10 than their unselected cohorts. Therefore, look for all 10 activities, and then compare your treatment with that of your peers. If your boss is investing in your career, you should encourage this process and stimulate its growth. If, on the other hand, your boss is not investing in your career, you need to develop a plan to foster this investment. The next chapter discusses some things that you should know in order to put such a plan together.

Summary

Your boss can help make you a fast tracker in at least 10 ways. Ask yourself whether your boss is doing these things with you.

Exercise. Are You on the Fast Track?

1. Does your boss provide you with special information through which you can learn company strategies?

2. Does your boss expose you to some of the various aspects of other departments?

3. Does your boss give you challenging assignments?

4. Does your boss discuss or show your strengths when talking to higher management?

5. Does your boss prepare you for difficult situations?

6. Does your boss advise you on long-range career plans?

7. Does your boss delegate important responsibilities to you when his or her workload is heavy?

8. Does your boss advise you on promotion opportunities?

9. Does your boss serve as your confidant on career problems?

10. Does your boss include your input in decisions for which only the boss is responsible?

To ride the fast track in your organization, you must have your boss invest in your career. Learn to recognize the investment process in order to take advantage of your opportunities and to reciprocate your boss's investments. Encourage your immediate supervisor's active participation in your development. Your boss may misread your potential and overlook you as a good career investment. Bosses often make mistakes of this kind, particularly if the subordinate waits passively to be discovered. Don't let yourself be overlooked. Right now, find out whether you're riding the fast track; don't wait too long to find out you were on the wrong track. Your career is too important to entrust to others.

Getting your boss to notice your potential is your first hurdle. Once you've surmounted that hurdle, and you have your boss's attention, you can begin the negotiation process to manage your career. This negotiation may be delicate for you, especially if your boss has never done it before; the next section of this book tells you how to do it successfully. If you find that you're not on the fast track already, you can use these tactics to get on it. Once you know you're on the fast track, you can use these tactics to make sure that you stay on it.

4

How to Get on the Fast Track

In Chapter 3, you were shown the crucial importance of getting your boss to invest in the future of your career. You were warned that without this investment, it would be very difficult indeed to get onto the fast track. And you were shown several ways for discerning whether your boss was investing in your career's future or merely training you to be effective in your present job. You were even given a few hints on how to make it worth your boss's while to invest in your career. But you weren't shown (a) what your boss looks for when deciding how much to invest in a subordinate, (b) what insiders do to show leadership in outgrowing their present jobs, and (c) how career investment leads to career success. Read on.

What Bosses Say They Look For

My associates and I asked 100 bosses from two manufacturing companies what characteristics (a) of their subordinates and (b) of their working relationships with their subordinates helped them decide in whom to invest. (See Table 4.1 for comparative statistics on subordinates who were and who were not selected for advancement.) Here are the top three answers:

Table 4.1 What Bosses Look For

	Percentage of Subordinates Described by This Characteristic	
Characteristic	Selected	Unselected
Make similar decisions	68%	25%
Dependable assistance in crises	85%	50%
Effective working relationship	88%	65%

1. Given the same complex problems, this subordinate and I will make the same decision. For example,

- We see the situation of the company, its markets, and its constituents similarly.
- We tend to think alike on important business issues.
- We have compared notes on previous complex problems, and I have developed confidence in the compatibility of our methods for solving problems.

2. In an emergency, I can count on this subordinate to complete an assignment I started. For example,

- This subordinate is dependable and will not let me down when I really need him or her.
- This subordinate has the ability and confidence to step into an emergency.
- This subordinate has helped in crises in the past, and I have confidence that he or she would do it again when necessary.

3. My working relationship with this person is effective. For example,

- We communicate effectively and coordinate our efforts efficiently.
- We collaborate well in our work by exchanging required resources.

- We have developed a mutually effective and rewarding working relationship.

Bosses invest in subordinates who make similar decisions, are dependable, and share effective working relationships with them. Even when two subordinates have the same promotion potential, a boss may select just one for individual development.

How it Works

Here is how people are selected for career investment. Suppose a manager, Lee Wong, has four subordinates reporting directly to him. Imagine also that Lee assesses these four people, as shown in Table 4.2. Mary Wynkowski is rated high on decision-making similarity, dependability, and collaborative relationship; Bill Ramirez is rated low on decision similarity, but high on dependability, and average on collaboration; Steve Stanton is average on decision similarity and collaboration, and low on dependability; Pam Romano is low on all three.

In addition to fulfilling the normal managerial responsibilities for his department, Lee spends some time each week investing in his subordinates' careers. Naturally, Lee seeks to invest in those with the most potential. Thus, of the time and energy that Lee sets aside for this function, he invests most of his attention in Mary. Because

Table 4.2 Investment of a Manager's Attention in Individual Members

	Assessment of Subordinates			
Manager's Evaluation	Mary	Bill	Steve	Pam
Characteristic being assessed				
Similarity of decisions	High	Low	Average	Low
Dependability	High	High	Low	Low
Collaborative relationship	High	Average	Average	Low
Proportion of available time, energy, and resources to invest	50%	25%	15%	10%

she already excels in her present job, he focuses on helping Mary to continue to outgrow her present job. Bill receives the next-largest share of Lee's attention, during which Lee focuses on training Bill to make more appropriate decisions and to work more effectively with Lee. Steve demonstrates only average abilities, so he uses a small amount of his time training Steve to become more dependable. Nonetheless, Steve still receives a bit more attention than Pam, who is rated low on all three characteristics. All subordinates require at least a minimum amount of a manager's attention, so Pam receives exactly the minimum of Lee's attention, during which he attempts to train her to come up to the average in all areas.

When managers were asked to rate their investments in their selected people (e.g., Mary) and their high-potential but unselected people (e.g., Bill), they placed the selected people on a fast development track relative even to the second-place people. (The training invested in others [e.g., Steve and Pam] was discussed in Chapter 3.)

How can you increase your chances of being selected by your boss? Milton Schloss, retired chairman of Sara Lee and of John Morrell (food processing corporations), and noted developer of executive talent, suggests the following:

• Learn about your organization beyond your job.
• Tell your boss that you want extra work.
• Make your boss look good.
• Give your boss credit in front of others.
• Take an interest in your boss, your boss's family, and your boss's career without being obvious about it.

Note: The way to show a personal interest in your boss without being obvious about it is to show interest in all the people with whom you work. Make a study of all the people on whom you depend for your work and for your information, or who depend on you for your work. Particularly show an interest in the motivations of the people with whom and around whom you work. Later in this chapter, you'll see added benefits of developing personal interaction skills, and Chapter 6 addresses these issues specifically.

What Fast-Track Managers Do

My research partners and I wanted to find out just how fast-track managers had demonstrated their intentions to outgrow their present jobs. So we asked more than a thousand line managers (from department heads to management trainees) in five leading corporations about both their working relationships and about what they did to show leadership in their jobs. We found that they did more of the following 13 activities than did their slow-track colleagues. These suggestions also apply equally well to managers-to-be.

1. Demonstrate initiative to get things moving
2. Attempt to exercise leadership to make the unit more effective
3. Show a willingness to take risks to accomplish assignments
4. Strive to add to the value of assignments
5. Actively seek out new job assignments for self-improvement
6. Persist on a valuable project after others give up
7. Build networks to extend capability
8. Influence others by doing something extra
9. Deal constructively with ambiguity
10. Seek exposure to managers outside the home division
11. Apply technical training on the job, and build on that training to develop broader expertise.
12. Work to build and maintain a close working relationship with the immediate supervisor
13. Work to get the immediate supervisor promoted

The following examples illustrate how each of these actions enabled these subordinates to become fast-track managers.

1. Demonstrate Initiative. By demonstrating initiative, subordinates make their boss aware that they are eager to outgrow their jobs. For example, fast-track subordinates may demonstrate initiative by identifying problem areas in their jobs and then acting to correct the problems. Thus, when Johan Meier sees a problem with a customer order and handles the problem the way he has seen his manager handle it before (even though this is not part of his job description), he is indicating to his boss that he is capable of and willing to take on added responsibilities.

2. Exercise Leadership. An important characteristic of fast-track managers is that they are able to exercise leadership when necessary. Susan Dixon shows this by helping her co-workers perform their jobs more efficiently and by providing direction when her co-workers are not certain as to the best method to use. In addition, Susan attempts to exercise leadership by offering to take charge of special projects, such as interdepartmental task forces, which will help to develop her leadership skills. Chapter 9 offers suggestions for aspiring leaders.

3. Take Risks. In Chapter 1, Secret 3 urged you to take career risks by being willing to make tough decisions. This need to take risks increases as managers reach higher levels in the organization. Similarly, those managers who are going to be successful in the organization are willing to take risks in their dealings with their boss and co-workers. One way managers may do this is by communicating to their supervisor the problems in the work unit, soliciting advice or added resources, as needed, even though pressure in the work group dictates that this is not done. Similarly, they may take risks by supporting issues that they believe are correct, even though others in the work unit may not support the issue. In addition, fast-track managers are not afraid to talk about their mistakes. Rather, they use past follies to their advantage by indicating to others what they have learned from their mistakes.

4. Add Value. Fast-track managers are constantly looking for opportunities to grow in their jobs. They find that one of the best ways to do this is to make their work more challenging and meaningful. For example, in his job as a supervisor of a market research department, Bill Atsuta found that unless he added value to his work, his job became boring and repetitive and didn't allow him to develop his skills. Thus, rather than just monitoring the performance of the telephone interviewers, as his job description suggested, he added value to his job by offering his managers input as to how interviews could be conducted more effectively, and he wrote un-solicited reports to those in charge of the development of the interviews that identified problem areas and suggestions for improvement. As a result of his extra effort, Bill found himself promoted to department head and on his way to the fast track.

5. Self-improvement Assignment. Rather than waiting for their bosses to offer them opportunities, fast-track managers seek opportunities on their own to make the most out of not only their jobs but also themselves. Thus, these managers look for opportunities that will allow them to develop their skills and to grow on their jobs. They may request special training or take on assignments that require them to use new skills. They may also ask their managers to indicate their strengths and weaknesses so that they may improve in their areas of weakness.

6. Persist on a Project. To get on the fast track, Mark Conaton has always had a policy of being a go-getter. If an assignment appears to be going nowhere, he pauses a moment in order to view the assignment in a new way. Then he uses the three-phased problem-solving strategy described in Chapter 7, thus providing new direction in the task. If this strategy leads to failure, which in some cases it does, he assesses the situation to find out what went wrong, and he uses the mistake as an opportunity for learning. Perhaps most important, Mark has learned never to make the same mistake twice.

7. Build Networks. In Chapter 1, Secret 8 introduced the idea of competence networks. For Jean Roberti, getting on the fast track meant making as many contacts as possible in her field and, in particular, contacts with those in her competence network. She made it a point to always find out what was going on in the organization and who was responsible for getting work done. She then initiated relationships with these people, which involved offering to do them favors or providing them with information that would help them in their positions. By building credits with the people in this network, she was thus able to obtain resources that would not have been possible without the others' help. Chapter 6 describes more fully how to identify, join, and build competence networks.

8. Influence Others. Influencing others is not as easy as it may appear. It involves building credibility, as well as adjusting your interpersonal style to match those of others. In his job at an advertising agency, Jim Lubinski seemed to have a real knack for doing just this. Well known as the best ad writer in his department, others often came to him for advice. Jim took special care to deal with the problems of each person individually. Thus, when Jim wanted something in return, others were more than willing to comply with his requests. By building these exchanges, Jim found that he had a lot of influence in his department. Chapters 6 and 9 describe how you can develop and use this influence to manage your career.

9. Resolve Ambiguity. One of the most difficult problems for managers in organizations is learning how to deal with ambiguity because ambiguity characterizes many of the difficult situations people face in the work place. Frequently, it's unclear what's not working, why it's not working, or what's needed in order to make things work. Also, people in the workplace may present ambiguous requests or offer ambiguous rationales. Those managers who learn how to handle these ambiguous situations most effectively find themselves on the fast track. When Tony Steiner found himself working with a boss who was always very ambiguous in his requests, Tony took several steps to deal with the ambiguity rather than simply becoming frustrated and not completing the assignments. Perhaps most importantly, he took the initiative to gather as much information as possible—from his supervisor, peers, and others. When necessary, he made educated assumptions that allowed him to continue the task. Throughout the process, he approached his boss for brief feedback on whether he was performing the assignment properly. By using his knowledge and best judgment, Tony was able to complete ambiguous tasks while requiring very little of his supervisor's time, and thus made himself a valuable assistant to the boss.

10. Seek Wider Exposure. Because information is such a powerful resource in organizations, managers who aspire to the fast track actively seek ways to gather more information. One way to do this is by associating with managers outside the home division. By interacting with outside managers, potential fast-track managers gain a better understanding of their organization and its operations, as well as the different problems faced by members of other departments.

Though she worked in the accounting department of her organization, Janice Lindsay often ate lunch with friends who worked in other areas, such as marketing, personnel, and production. In her conversations with these friends about their jobs, she learned about the organization in ways that others in the accounting department had not. Thus, if others in her department, including her boss, needed information about happenings in the organization, they went to Janice. By establishing herself as an information source, Janice increased her potential to influence others.

11. Build up and on Existing Skills. In Chapter 1, Secret 9 suggests that you avoid competence traps. This does *not*, however suggest that you do not build on and expand existing skills. When new managers enter organizations, they have a certain amount of knowledge and technical skills that make them desirable to the organization. Often, however, this technical training is limited, and within a relatively short period of time, it may become obsolete. Thus, managers must continually work to keep their technical skills current. For example, Elizabeth Chen was hired because she was an expert on the organization's computer system. Realizing the value of her technical expertise, she began immediately to learn about other computer systems. Thus, when the organization decided to change computer systems, Elizabeth's usefulness in the organization continued to grow because she had foreseen the change and had prepared herself by acquiring training on the new system. By ensuring that she was adequately trained to handle the technical aspects of her job, Elizabeth made herself a valuable asset to her boss and her co-workers.

12. Develop a Close Working Relationship with the Boss. As was made clear in Part I, one of the most powerful influences on your career progress is your boss. Your boss controls the types of opportunities and resources, as well as the types of rewards, you will receive from the organization. It is vital that you strive to develop the best working relationship possible with your boss.

To develop a good relationship with his boss, Greg Brackman

initiated as much interaction as possible with his boss. He avoided "being obvious" about his interest in the boss by showing interest in his co-workers as well. By offering to do favors for his boss or to provide information that his boss needed, he made his boss aware of his willingness to help out when needed. In addition, by completing assignments in the manner the boss desired and by learning to think like the boss, Greg established himself as a valuable trusted assistant. In exchange for his effort, Greg was then able to obtain favors from his boss, which eventually led to a promotion and a head start onto the fast track.

13. Promote the Boss. In Chapter 1, Secret 6 showed that the best way to get to the fast track may be to work toward promoting your boss: Do your job the best you can so that you help make your boss look good. Then, when your boss advances through the organization, your boss will take you along. In her position as an assistant store manager of a restaurant franchise, Becky Stagnaro did everything she could to make her store as profitable as possible (worked late hours, took on special assignments, etc.) even though her store manager received all the credit for the excellent management of the store. When her manager was promoted to become the district manager, he recommended Becky to fill his empty position. Thus, by working to promote her boss, Becky was able to move into his position when it became empty, and, at the same time, she had a very supportive contact at the district manager level.

Outgrow Your Present Job

These activities all require you to grow out of the narrow confines of your job by assuming greater personal responsibility, by taking larger risks, and by growing more quickly professionally. Your boss notices these activities that make a difference to your career. Your participation in these activities communicates your readiness for career investment. Once you are noticed as a candidate for investment, additional opportunities for experiences likely will be forthcoming. Chapters 5, 6, and 7 describe how to capitalize on these opportunities to both fulfill your career aspirations and prove yourself worthy of future career investments.

Job Experiences: How Investment Leads to the Fast Track

Study of Which Job Experiences Lead to the Fast Track

How does career investment lead to greater career progress? The answer to this question is vital to career success. If people can recognize the ways in which investment provided job experiences that lead to the fast track, they can more actively control their careers. They can seek out career-enhancing experiences and avoid career-threatening mistakes.

To answer this question, my research partners and I randomly selected and studied the careers of 50 fast-track and 50 slow-track managers in an engineering division of a multinational consumer products corporation. The managers we studied were college graduates with at least 5 (and as many as 15) years service with the company. They represented all levels of the management hierarchy.

When we focused on the managers' first four jobs after joining the organization, we found that seven types of job experiences were much more common for the fast-track managers than for their slow-track colleagues:

1. They received career investments from at least one immediate superior
2. Careers were influenced in a positive manner by an average of four superiors
3. They gained technical expertise from several superiors
4. They learned how to influence others, including team leadership, from several superiors
5. Their career development was opportunistic and active regarding specific job experience
6. They moved to different job assignments at appropriate intervals
7. They applied their education and training in their first job

Clearly, the first four of the seven kinds of job experiences depend entirely on having at least one superior invest in the subordinate's career during the first four job assignments. Even the fifth, sixth, and seventh job experiences also rely heavily on being offered the opportunity to gain those experiences. For a subordinate to gain these job experiences, the subordinate had to get at least one superior to invest substantially in her or his career.

Further, we found that managers who did not receive these job experiences during the first four job assignments were unlikely to be in the fast-track group later. Those who experienced the selected treatment at least once during their first four job assignments tended to be more successful years later than those who were never selected. This suggests that early growth experiences are especially relevant to later career progress. These early job experiences may show at least a few of the ways that a boss's career investment can launch a subordinate onto the fast track.

Engineering Career Choices

The differentiating effects of early job experiences can be seen in the case of Simone Piret and Giuseppe Purpura. Simone and Giuseppe were both highly rated graduates of one of the finest engineering colleges in the country, and both joined the company 12 years ago. However, their careers diverged drastically after the first 6 years. Today, Simone is the director of design engineering and a candidate for early promotion—a fast-tracker, while Giuseppe is one level below the director in another division and has reached his full potential—a slow-tracker.

Simone and Giuseppe began their careers in the company with comparable promise, training, and ambition: They were equally good bets to make the director level. Unfortunately for Giuseppe, his promise, training, and ambition were not enough. His faith in the public mask of written rules and job descriptions, and his ignorance of the hidden face of the unwritten rules and hidden strategies in his organization led him to make a series of poor career choices.

In contrast, fortunately for Simone, her promise, training, and ambition were augmented by recognizing hidden-face opportunities that allowed her to make a series of excellent career choices. Let us consider how Simone and Giuseppe developed opportunities and reacted to offers during their first three years on the job.

Starting Out Together. Before their first day on the job, both Simone and Giuseppe had been told that in this company, fast-track people receive their first promotion on the first anniversary of their joining the company and slow-track people receive it up to nine months later. In addition, their second promotion should arrive on their third anniversary if they are on the fast track, but later if they are on the slow track. Moreover, they were told, the faster the promotions are received, the better for their careers. Unfortunately, this rule is only partly accurate. Both Simone and Giuseppe were promoted on their first anniversary, but Giuseppe received his second promotion nine months before Simone did.

Where Simone's Path Diverged. During the first year, both Simone and Giuseppe applied themselves to learning their new jobs and the public mask of their company. Both developed equally well and learned the company's unique way of doing things. Both were potential fast-trackers. About nine months into their second year, Simone's supervisor asked her if she would be interested in working on a project that cut across several different disciplines. This assignment required that she learn about these new disciplines. She asked her supervisor how this might affect her career progress. She was told that it might slow her down temporarily, but that he thought this new knowledge would make her a more well-rounded professional in the division. She then jumped at the opportunity.

Although this new learning delayed her second promotion by nine months, it opened several new career paths for her. Because she had worked with many colleagues in different departments and had acquired both interdepartmental expertise and working relationships, she was a valuable contributor to many subsequent interdisciplinary projects. In addition, she learned from different bosses in each of the various departments with whom she worked. Initially, they emphasized the technical expertise that she must acquire, but later they stressed the expertise of project team leadership.

On each assignment, she learned to perform beyond expectations and to seek new ways to contribute. She came to treat each project as her own and to do what was necessary to make it successful. When it became apparent that new expertise was required by a project, she would seek that expertise. She learned how to get the best results from her team members, even when she was a more junior member of the team. Project managers who had worked with her asked for her assistance on new projects. She came to be known as a person who could get things done.

What Simone Did Right. Consider Simone's development over the first four years in relation to the fast track opportunities listed on page 88. Simone's career development was opportunistic and active regarding specific job experiences. At each stage, she discovered what learning she needed and how to acquire it. She did not lock herself into learning more and more about less and less and thus become overly specialized. An immediate superior invested in her career, which opened the door to more career opportunities. Her career profited from the contributions of several bosses. She learned technical expertise from earlier bosses, and team and individual leadership skills from later bosses. Although she generally moved to different job assignments at appropriate intervals, she was not promoted until she had learned all she could from her present jobs.

What Giuseppe Did Wrong. Where did Giuseppe go wrong during his second and third year? In spite of his second promotion being earlier than Simone's, Giuseppe made several ill-advised choices during his second and third years. When his immediate superior asked Giuseppe if he would be interested in an interdisciplinary project, Giuseppe respectfully declined. His game plan was to become very good in one discipline and not waste time learning the work of other departments. He knew exactly which jobs were on his career ladder, and he figured that if he were as expert as the current incumbent of that job, that would be sufficient. In short, he believed the written job descriptions and the written job specifications.

Giuseppe quickly became a specialist in his discipline, both in expertise and in attitude. He was excellent on his drafting board, but he was not interested in how ideas got to him or what happened to them after they left him. Projects were someone else's concern. All he wanted was to be told his assignment in detail. He did not appreciate project directors who would change his assignment several times. The better Giuseppe became at his specialty, the less patience he demonstrated with changes. Although Giuseppe had not learned either team or individual leadership, he was promoted early to a supervisory position based on his specialized expertise.

Despite his earlier second promotion, Giuseppe failed to capitalize on several of the fast-track opportunities he was offered: First, he did not allow his immediate superiors to invest in his career, because he was convinced that if he did his public-mask job in an outstanding manner and did not get distracted by other activities going on in a project, his promotions would be assured. Second, his career development was not opportunistic and active—he locked into a specific and passive plan. His career paths were limited to his immediate career ladder: subsection, section, department, group, and division. Third, Giuseppe never learned team or individual leadership from the experts, and this lack was the primary reason for his career's premature plateauing. He failed to identify and join competence networks, he didn't give people the credit that they deserved, and he never admitted his own mistakes. Finally, he didn't move to different job assignments at appropriate intervals. In fact, he moved too little laterally and too fast vertically—he was promoted to supervisor before he had learned all he needed to in order to outgrow his previous job.

What Were the Key Differences? Simone learned some of the unwritten rules and hidden strategies early in her career that Giuseppe has not learned yet, and Simone is still enjoying her trip on the fast track that Giuseppe fell off in his fourth year. The crucial unwritten rules that Giuseppe failed to recognize were based on one key secret of leadership within organizations:

> To be effective in an organization, you must learn how to effectively involve others in helping you to be effective.

Giuseppe mistakenly believed that his individual competence and expertise would be sufficient to keep him on the fast track. He was wrong. As Simone realized early in her career, her own competence would not be enough to take her beyond the lower rungs of management. To be effective, she needed to actively enlist the support and enthusiasm of others. As a manager, Giuseppe was ineffective in interacting and collaborating with others, so for the integrated collaborative work of the organization, he was unable to achieve results. Unfortunately, he, his subordinates, his co-workers, and the organization suffered as a consequence.

How Fast-Track Managers Interact

Interpersonal Interaction Style. In addition to the 13 actions, fast-track managers clearly must have excellent interpersonal skills. Strong interpersonal skills lead to having numerous interpersonal working relationships, which usually allow people to increase their influence in their work unit.

Thus, in order to persuasively influence others, good interpersonal skills are a must. Part of these good interpersonal skills involves being sensitive to the different behavioral styles of their co-workers and then adjusting their own interpersonal style to the style of the other person. For example, when Jimmie is attempting to influence Caitlin, who is shy and sensitive, he would take a much softer approach than he would with Sue, who is very confident and ambitious. By recognizing and adjusting the manner in which he deals with others, Jimmie's attempts to gain influence over his co-workers are much more successful.

Credibility. One key to fruitful interpersonal interactions is credibility. For some people, establishing credibility comes easily. For example, Caitlin is a proven expert in her field, applied laser technology, so she doesn't have much trouble establishing credibility and encouraging others in the technical division to do as she suggests. On the other hand, Jimmie, who has not yet demonstrated this expertise, has found it more difficult to establish credibility by these means. Thus, Jimmie has had to develop strong interpersonal skills in order to provide reasons for others to listen to him.

Jimmie also establishes his credibility by building interpersonal contacts into a competence network—the "who you know" method. Because his contacts are respected members of his field and his industry, then others are impressed by the contacts' interest and belief in his potential to perform.

In addition, the manner in which Jimmie deals with his co-workers affects how much credibility they give him. He shows that he respects others' knowledge and ability by influencing them but not dominating or overpowering them. One of the fastest ways to lose credibility is by threatening someone else's. He's always careful not to treat others as if they don't know what they're doing. Instead, he builds his credibility by helping others to prove their own ability.

A proven track record may also help Jimmie to establish his credibility with others. For example, he can prove himself gradually through successful work experiences. In many ways, an impressive track record establishes more credibility than written qualifications do.

Exercise. Are You Moving to the Fast Track?

Ask yourself the following questions. For any "no" responses you give, think about how this might siderail you off the fast track. Then try to think of some strategies for changing your answer to "yes." Ask trusted peers—or even your boss—for suggestions on how to improve your chances of getting onto the fast track.

1. Do you and your boss tend to agree about managerial decisions?

2. Can your boss count on you to complete assignments, particularly if your boss has a crisis and needs your help?

3. Do you and your boss have an effectively close collaborative working relationship?

4. Do you take the time to learn about your organization beyond the boundaries of your present job?

5. Do you ask your boss for extra, challenging assignments?

6. Does your performance of your work make your boss look good?

7. Do you give your boss and your co-workers credit for their work and their help in front of other people?

8. Do you show an interest in your boss and in your co-workers?

9. Do you take the initiative in moving projects forward?

10. Do you show leadership in making your work unit more effective?

11. Are you willing to take educated risks in order to do your work well?

12. Do you give something extra to add to the value of your work?

13. Do you actively seek assignments that will improve your skills and increase your knowledge?

14. Do you persist in looking for ways to handle troublesome but important situations and projects?

15. Are you using strong interpersonal skills to develop credibility and to build strong collaborative relationships?

16. Are you able to use your collaborative relationships and your credibility to influence others in your work unit?

17. Do you handle ambiguity effectively?

18. Do you reach outside your own work unit to form collaborative relationships and to learn more about the organization?

19. Do you use and continue to develop your technical expertise on your job?

20. Do you work to get your boss promoted?

Do Co-workers Know?

Do the co-workers of the people involved know about the different quality of the boss–subordinate relationships? In a large government agency, workers, their bosses, and their co-workers agreed quite well on the quality of these working relationships. Clearly, the different quality of an effective boss–subordinate collaborative relationship is visible to peers within the same work unit, as well as to the bosses and workers involved.

Although boss, peers, and the workers involved agree on the different quality of relationships between subordinates and bosses, no one includes this information in written documents. People recognize these differences in working relationships, but don't look for this information in a company manual. Rather, judge it from looking at how people work together over time.

Summary

Bosses invest in selected individual's careers. In choosing candidates, they look for three things:

1. A person that will tend to make the same decision as the boss would make.
2. A person that can be depended on to complete an assignment that the boss started.
3. A person who can develop an effective working relationship with the boss.

How this process works was described as investing a boss's scarcest resource—time—in different people's careers. Fast-track managers who developed trusted assistant relationships with their bosses did more of 13 specific activities (see pages 82–87) than their slow-track colleagues.

After establishing yourself on the fast track, your next task is to outgrow your present job. Chapter 5 shows you how to do that.

PART II

Securing Success: Using the Hidden Strategies

To Manage Your Career, Learn from Mistakes

The basic premise of this book is that only you can be the most effective manager of your own career. No one else can do it for you. But others can offer you guidance and assistance. For example, this book can be a useful resource in this endeavor, helping you to learn from the successes and failures of others.

Of course, you will still make mistakes. Everyone does. In fact, much of the inside information disclosed in this book was revealed by fast-trackers who had learned them the hard way—from having made some serious career blunders. The key difference between fast-trackers and slow-trackers is not the number or the severity of their errors, but whether they use their missteps as learning tools in order to profit from them. This book offers you the opportunity to learn from some mistakes the easy way—by observing the mishaps of others. What's more, you can also learn from their accomplishments. Though this book warns you of career hazards, it focuses on alerting you to opportunities for success.

97

Part I of this book taught you to learn to think about succeeding in your career in a new way. What you had learned previously from the written rules and the conventional strategies forms only a small part of what you need to understand in order to be effective. You must also discover and use the inside information. Techniques described in Part I will help you to make sense of the way things really get done in your organization.

Manage Your Career

Your challenge in Part II is to use some of this inside information to convince your superiors and your co-workers that you are a potential fast-tracker and that you will show gratifying pay-offs for their investments in your career. In Chapter 4, you'll learn specific behaviors for getting onto the fast track with the help of your supervisor. Chapter 5 describes the three-phased process by which you can rapidly outgrow your present job—and grow into a more responsible one.

Chapter 6 reveals how you can promote yourself, your supervisor, and your competent co-workers, by noticing, joining, building, and using collaborative networks. Though you must be in charge of managing your career, you will need to elicit the help and the resources of other people. Therefore, you need to learn not only how to manage your own career with the help of others but also how to earn their help.

One way to earn the aid of others is to solve problems collaboratively. Chapter 7 suggests ways of solving problems by involving the people who will participate in implementation of the solution. An effective three-phased method for solving problems may help you manage problems for a very worthwhile objective: the advancement of your career.

What You Will Gain

The introduction to Part I mentioned a few of the benefits that fast-trackers enjoy. Take a moment now to think about which of these is most important to you. Before you begin the chapters in Part II, ask yourself what you want to gain from riding on the fast track:

- Do you abhor feeling too many negative effects of on-the-job stress?
- Do you long to choose your own work assignments and to feel successful and competent in fulfilling them?
- Do you strive to make important contributions to the people in your environment?
- Do you relish mastering seemingly impossible challenges?
- Do you cherish being admired and appreciated by the people with whom you work?
- Do you lust after influence and power within your organization?
- Do you savor feeling that you're part of an insider network of people who do important work?
- Do you exult in feeling that you can get whatever resources and rewards you want for yourself, as well as for your work unit?

As you read the four chapters that follow, think about your own goals and how you can use these suggestions to help you reach them. These are your goals for your career. Guide your career to fulfill your dreams.

5

Outgrow Your Present Job

Recognizing a Dead End

Jo Ziegler took a job as an analyst with a large electronic data processing company and was assigned to a work unit responsible for an administrative computer system. The unit consisted of 5 analysts and Ed Conger, the boss. Jo was hired to replace Gordan Drazrik, a programmer who had suddenly quit a month before. Jo's first assignment was to improve the payroll system. It wasn't long before she was experiencing communication problems with Ed.

Ed set a firm, 30-day deadline for completion of the project. Jo worked very hard to understand the current system, although Gordy had kept inadequate records. Jo got cooperation from the other analysts, but she found it difficult to get information from Ed, who always seemed preoccupied. So Jo was forced to take work home on weekends and often stayed late at the office on weekdays. She found many inefficiencies in the current program and asked Ed if it was all right to change them. Ed told her, "I don't care what you do as long as it's up and running on budget and on time!"

Jo felt that she was working far beyond her job description, but she kept trying to make the payroll system the best it could be, given the time and budget constraints. Amazingly, Jo's new program was completed on time and on budget—a resounding success for the company and for Ed's unit. The new features made it much easier to use the system.

Ed received many appreciative memos from other managers in the company. There was even talk of a possible promotion for Ed. Only Jo's work-unit colleagues and a few other system users were aware of her contribution. Jo began to feel frustrated. Ed had not even said thank you!

Jo also wanted to work on a new project that was still unassigned; this would allow her to improve her skills on a system she was not familiar with. But when she asked for the opportunity, Ed refused to collaborate. Instead, Ed began to outline Jo's next assignment—another repair job. Jo was stunned. What had gone wrong?

Jo assumed she wasn't communicating effectively with Ed, so she kept trying. Over the next few months, the situation got worse. Jo asked Ed's advice on certain points of the new project, but Ed only expressed irritation at Jo's "dependence" on him. Finally, Jo asked to be transferred out of Ed's unit and she decided to leave the company if the transfer was refused. She even started to search the want ads.

Jo had realized that Ed was not going to invest in helping her get on the fast track. Without Ed's support, she was not going to be able to outgrow her present job and move up within the company. Given that, she decided to learn all she could within her present job until she could find something better either within the organization or elsewhere. To help keep herself focused on her long-term goals instead of her short-term frustrations, she made a list of things she'd do to get the most out of her present job.

If you ever find yourself in a dead-end job or stranded on a sinking ship (e.g., your organization is in trouble, despite the efficiency of your work unit), you might use a similar list to help get the most from a bad situation. Meanwhile, use your contacts with others to lead you to contacts within organizations. Most people get hired through just these kinds of contacts.

Once you're in a job that offers you opportunities for growth, it's time to start outgrowing it. Chapter 4 described what bosses look for when deciding to invest in one or two of their subordinates, as well as how these investments lead to job experiences that help subordinates outgrow their present jobs. In this chapter, you'll discover three phases you move through in order to outgrow your job.

Exercise.

1. Find out more about this organization—
   a. What innovations have they developed in this industry?
   b. What products and services do they provide well?
   c. How do they do the things they do well?
   d. What mistakes have people made in this organization?
   e. How could these mistakes have been avoided?
   f. How are decisions made, and who makes them?
   g. What do they have problems with?
   h. How might these problems be solved?

2. Find out more about my co-workers—
   a. Who really understands the organization and knows how it works?
   b. Who can I count on to do their work well so that my work comes out better?
   c. Who counts on me to do a good job in order to do their jobs well?
   d. Who might know people in this organization or elsewhere who might be contacts for a new job?
   e. Who has the best access to which of the organization's resources?

3. Find out about my job—
   a. What other skills should I develop in this job that might help me in the future?
   b. What other equipment and systems should I become familiar with that might help me later?
   c. What other knowledge or expertise should I develop here that might help me in the future wherever I go?

Three Phases of Outgrowing Your Job

This process of growing out of your job follows a sequence of phases from (1) role-finding to (2) role-making to (3) role-implementation. *Role-finding* is concerned with uncovering the hidden features of your job situation. Employing the methods discussed in Chapter 2, you search for the unwritten rules of your job, of your co-workers and their jobs, and of your job environment. After role-finding, you begin *role-making*, which involves negotiating an initial set of understandings with your co-workers about your job situation. Finally, after role-making, you begin *role-implementation*. This phase involves working out over time a set of mature understandings about your job situation.

Phase 1—Role-Finding: Show Your Motivation and Your Ability

Fortunately for the organization, Jo was allowed to transfer to Solomon Cohen's unit—applying computer solutions to public administration settings. She now realizes how management should operate. Solomon has accepted her as a protégé and has begun the development process. Jo was delighted with her new and challenging assignments and the support, attention, and expert advice she receives from Solomon. She also became more productive, more creative, and more committed to her work and her work unit than she ever imagined she would be.

Jo's interactions with Solomon were different from her interactions with Ed in a number of subtle ways. Solomon used hidden strategies, which allowed Jo to grow out of the narrow confines of her written job description.

Solomon employs fast-track leadership (described in Part III) with his people. When Jo joined his unit, Solomon began the role-finding phase with her and she with him. Solomon had many questions about Jo's recent interactions with Ed. He knew Ed quite well and admired his technical expertise. He began the process by offering Jo small but challenging assignments to see how she would perform. He wondered whether she really sought to outgrow her job and whether his investment in her career would be profitable for him. On her part, Jo was questioning whether Solomon would reciprocate her investment or would she experience a repeat of her disappointment with Ed.

Three Questions Each

Three questions Solomon was attempting to answer during this role-finding phase were the following:

1. What tasks can Jo grow into beyond her official (written) job duties?
2. What rewards did she expect in exchange for outgrowing her job?
3. Will the necessary investments in her career pay off?

The corresponding three questions Jo was asking herself were the following:

1. What tasks can I grow into that will be seen as valuable by Solomon?
2. What rewards do I expect in exchange for growing out of my job in this direction?
3. How can I make my boss's investment in my career pay off for both of us?

Jo discovered that Solomon secretly wished to build a business plan for his pet project—a new expert system. This computer system would aid public health counselors in making case decisions.

At the proper moment, Jo suggested to Solomon that she would like to begin building this business plan on her own. She outlined the resources that she needed, including Solomon's support and guidance. She explained that such an assignment would be a good learning experience, and the successful completion of the project would be her reward.

She was given the assignment and considerably more resources than she had requested. Solomon took great interest in the progress of the project. Moreover, he came to discuss a large number of other departmental issues with her. In time, it was clear that Solomon was investing in Jo's career.

Jo had helped Solomon answer his questions about her investment value in a creative manner. She identified a project that she could accomplish and that was valuable to Solomon. She specified her expected rewards and the payoff to Solomon. In addition, her presentation answered Solomon's investment questions admirably. This was an example of active role-finding—helping your boss answer questions about making an investment in you. Jo had found a way to get Solomon's attention and to demonstrate her value as a trusted assistant who sought to grow out of her job and to promote her boss.

Both Solomon and Jo answered their questions in ways that indicated that a mutual investment was a good course of action. Solomon's increasing investments in Jo's career were reciprocated in kind by Jo. This moved their relationship into the role-making phase, in which negotiation, rather than show-and-tell becomes the norm.

Phase 2—Role-Making: Use Resources to Outgrow Your Present Job

When the role-finding phase is nearly complete, role-making appears. During the role-making phase, you and your boss begin to define the nature of your working relationship. During role-finding, you have less latitude to suggest an assignment, although in the preceding example, Jo had suggested the project to Solomon. The project she suggested, however, was one she knew Solomon favored. While role-making, you can more freely suggest projects, but the test of role-making is performance on the project. Jo had done her homework thoroughly and requested the needed resources and support from Solomon. She was confident that she could do a good job with the proper resources and support. She understood the risk and accepted it as reasonable. Her reasoning was that Solomon would be pleased with whatever progress she was able to achieve because he really wanted someone to test his idea.

Role-making depends on the mutual investment of valued resources by both parties. Each party invests something the other party values, and each party sees the exchange as reasonable. The rules governing the exchange must be acceptable to both parties if it is to result in a high level of mutual trust. Table 5.1 compares the written rules and overt strategies of role-making with the unwritten rules and hidden strategies of this phase.

Exercise. Find Your Role

In Chapter 1 (pages 7–10), you made some notes on your job description. Take this description out, and review your answers, this time thinking in terms of your boss's perspective:

1. Which routine tasks could you outgrow that your boss would consider appropriate for you to discontinue?

2. How can you ensure that these tasks are done once you stop doing them?

3. Of those that you'd like to discontinue, but your boss might want to continue, how are you going to plan to outgrow them to your boss's satisfaction?

4. Which of your present tasks would your boss like to see you master more successfully?

5. Which of your other present tasks do you need to master as an investment in your own career's future?

6. Which of your boss's tasks and responsibilities would your boss like you to grow into?

7. Which of your boss's tasks and responsibilities could you handle well for your boss?

8. What resources do you need from your boss in order to grow in all of the foregoing ways?
   a. Time and energy from the boss
   b. Information and training from the boss
   c. Time, energy, information, or training from any of your co-workers (which must be taken from using these resources in other ways)
   d. Supplies
   e. Access to or use of equipment
   f. Office space or transportation or other resources

9. How will you ensure that your boss receives at least an equivalent exchange, if not a net gain, for investing these resources in you?

Your answers to these questions, and the actions you take as a result, should prepare you for the next phase: role-making.

Table 5.1 Role-Making Tasks

Overt Activities (Learning and Performing)	Hidden (Covert) Strategies (Finding, Making, Implementing)
1. Accept job responsibilities in job description?	Negotiate meaning of responsibilities with boss and others.
2. Accept job authority in job description?	Negotiate instrumental value of resources with boss and others.
3. Accept official operating procedures?	Negotiate operating procedures with boss and others.
4. Accept scheduled training programs?	Negotiate training opportunities with boss and others.
5. Accept compensation schedule?	Negotiate compensation with boss and others.
6. Accept formal objectives?	Negotiate priority objectives with boss and others.
7. Accept official accountability?	Negotiate meaning of accountability with boss and others.
8. Accept formal relations with other departments?	Negotiate relations with other departments with boss and others.
9. Accept official performance appraisal process?	Negotiate specific performance appraisal process with boss and others.

Proactively Exceeding the Written Standards

Kendall Washington, an automation engineer for a paper products corporation, described how he used the hidden strategies to discover how he could outgrow his job and move up the fast track. Ken's job involved working for a dozen different clients, as well as his boss. These clients were production managers at the different paper manufacturing plants across the country.

When Ken started this job, he first studied his job description, and then he talked with his boss and with each of his clients about how he could best serve his clients' needs. In this way, he began to negotiate the meaning of his responsibilities (as shown in Table

5.1). As part of these discussions, Ken asked about what his boss and his clients wanted him to do for them and what resources he should employ to do those things. They also talked about how they would like Ken to work with them. Using these discussions, he was able to work out different ways of serving the differing needs of his clients.

Ken thus used negotiation (discussions with his boss and with his clients) as a hidden strategy for accomplishing the overt activities of his role, regarding his objectives (item 6 in Table 5.1) accountability (7), relations with other departments (8), and performance appraisal (9). He continued to ask his clients and his boss if he was meeting their needs. For Ken's performance appraisal, Ken's boss interviewed each of his 12 clients about how he was serving their needs. He then put all of this information together to form a picture of Ken's performance.

Because Ken was keeping close tabs on his clients' needs and his boss's needs, he was always able to obtain the resources he needed in order to forge his own role. If his boss asked for a rationale for providing the resources, Ken was prepared with specific reasons, based on his analysis of his clients' needs. Very soon, his boss readily provided Ken with any of the resources he requested. Ken had effectively negotiated with his boss for the resources he needed. (Resource development is discussed more fully in Chapter 6.)

Ken didn't wait to see what things got rewarded in his organization. He was more proactive in getting this information and acting on it before it was too late. He had served the needs of his 12 clients and his boss extremely well, and he knew it. Ken didn't simply follow the exact dictates of written policies and job descriptions. Thus, Ken wasn't surprised by a very high performance appraisal. If, instead, he had followed the written guidelines too closely, he might have been unhappily surprised by a negative performance appraisal. Had he failed to go beyond this to the hidden strategies, he might not have kept track of how his clients were evaluating his performance. If you work directly with clients, follow Ken's example and monitor the changing needs of your clients.

The point here is that much that is required for effective performance requires you to go beyond the written rules, to find the hidden ones. Moreover, the unwritten rules contain career opportunities never even mentioned in public documents and statements.

Based on their success in various ventures on the job, they worked out reasonably efficient and effective ways of working as a team. Over time, Ken and his boss worked out the details of their working relationship and moved to the final phase—that of role implementation.

Tough Negotiations

Jawaharlal Shankar, an assistant department manager of a savings and loan association, complained that Kia Pao, his manager, would not listen to his request for the support he needed in order to effectively assist her. Though Jawaharlal's job description did not specify this role, he was managing the office. Kia was totally engaged in developing new business, though she was formally in charge of managing the office. Further, Kia did not share critical information with Jawaharlal or include him in important decisions. He was forced to spend a lot of time finding out from others what was happening in his own department.

Jawaharlal decided that his need for resources was reasonable, so he asked to meet with Kia. At the meeting, each of them revealed a different interpretation of their common working relationship. Kia maintained that Jawaharlal really didn't need the information to do his job. Although she admitted that she didn't share even one half of the information with Jawaharlal, she didn't understand why he needed more than he was given. After all, she was the manager and he was only her assistant. In contrast, Jawaharlal asserted that he was effectively managing every function except new business development, and he needed this information.

Jawaharlal understood and was pleased that he had outgrown his job and was doing a large part of Kia's job. Kia was also pleased with Jawaharlal's growth and had gladly given him this opportunity. However, Kia had failed to appreciate the level of support required to do his new work.

Jawaharlal's first hurdle was to get Kia to focus on his situation. Jawaharlal asked Kia to meet with him for one hour each week in order to review Jawaharlal's situation. Jawaharlal carefully prepared for each of these meetings, writing an agenda that covered the items he needed to discuss. Kia's role was to understand what Jawaharlal was doing and how he would use the information that he requested.

Jawaharlal made the most of his one-hour meeting each week. He did his homework for each meeting and used the meeting time effectively, always ending the meetings on time or early.

Kia gradually became aware that Jawaharlal was a critical asset to her department and that he required investment from Kia to become an even more valuable contributor. Kia was not trying to exploit Jawaharlal's drive, but she had been distracted by her total involvement in new business development. All her attention was so focused on new business programs that she failed to consider Jawaharlal's situation.

Kia and Jawaharlal's early meetings covered what he did, what resources he needed from Kia, and how he would use these resources. Later meetings were devoted to Jawaharlal's career development and what he needed to learn. Jawaharlal learned how to negotiate effectively with Kia, even though she had superior power and status.

Kia gradually learned what it meant to develop Jawaharlal as her replacement. She derived great satisfaction from her sales activities, she was good at it, and she knew it. Nonetheless, she also had to ensure that the office was managed effectively.

Over time, they worked out how Jawaharlal would help her run the office with the support from Kia that he required. Kia would concentrate on new business and gradually train Jawaharlal in sales.

At first, in the role-making process, Jawaharlal was given only half of the career opportunities discussed in Chapter 3—the added responsibilities. He was not given the needed support, resources, and incentive. Kia failed to reciprocate for her good fortune in having Jawaharlal to help her with the office functions. These functions would have kept her from her first love—sales. However, to receive these benefits meant that she needed to invest in Jawaharlal's career. Once she understood the transactional nature of the process, she came to enjoy the exchanges. She came to recognize (a) that she could exchange career investments in Jawaharlal for exceptional efforts by him and (b) that this arrangement was profitable for both of them.

Not all bosses require this kind of active negotiation—Ken's boss was much more ready to offer the resources Ken needed. However, be prepared to do some negotiating for the resources you need in order to provide your boss with the assistance your boss needs.

Once you and your boss work through these negotiations and collaborate for a while, you'll be ready to move into the role implementation phase.

Phase 3—Role-Implementing: Learn to Collaborate Effectively

In the implementation phase, you and your boss refine the collaborative arrangement that the two of you negotiated in the role-making phase. As you work together on various projects, you make changes in the way you work together, and your relationship matures. You explore new areas of collaboration as your capabilities are enhanced and as new opportunities appear in your work.

Your working relationship matures from that of acquaintances to that of established team players. You develop mutual trust, respect, loyalty, and understanding. As your relationship matures, you no longer treat each other as mere acquaintances. Thus, equivalent exchanges become more appropriate than rewards and punishments.

Your relationship is transformed from simple exchange of self-interest outcomes to one of commitment to promoting each other's career through career-related learning and achieving superordinate goals. In other words, something larger than immediate self-interest of both parties becomes the driving force of the team. This system offers the payoffs of the fast track to both parties and specifies that the way to achieve these payoffs is to function as an effective mature team.

After the implementation phase, transactions may be incorporated into the formal documents of the organization in a number of ways. The transactions thus become part of the written, public organization. For example, you may receive a promotion, in which more responsibility is exchanged for higher status and higher pay. Formal, documented promotion routinely occurs as a result of role-making, following the negotiation that has already occurred within the working relationship (informal, unwritten guidelines).

Investment in Some Is Negotiated

Clearly, bosses develop different relationships with different subordinates, and these relationships lead to different career outcomes. But how does this get negotiated? To find out, we studied a company after a management reorganization had placed new people in almost all the direct reporting relationships in the company. We watched 200 managers and their supervisors build new management teams. (All bosses and managers were interviewed four times over the first nine months—first, fourth, seventh, and ninth month.)

We found that extremely dissimilar tracks emerged within the same unit. In fact, different managers followed different tracks in all of the work units studied. The working relationships studied ranged from the highest level ("trusted assistant") to the lowest level ("hired hand"), with many gradations between. The trusted assistant relationship was characterized by extremely high *quality* (trust, respect, loyalty, liking, intimacy, support, openness, and honesty) and a lot of investment and collaboration. The hired hand relationship was characterized by extremely low quality and almost no investment or collaboration.

Interestingly enough, we were able to predict the development of these relationships over nine months from information we collected during the *very first month* on the job, using questions about the quality of the early boss–manager exchange—their negotiations. People were placed on fast tracks or slow tracks very early in the process.

View from the Slow Track

By four months on the job, these managers complained about problems with getting needed information, being involved in important decisions, getting things done through their boss, and lack of cooperation among peers. Some were frequently surprised by changes in programs and procedures—they were the last to find out. Some were completely left out of critical decisions involving their sections, others were asked for some input but not really involved. Several experienced severe problems getting their bosses to use their authority to bail them out of problems or even to smooth the way when asked. Finally, a few complained about the lack of cooperation among people at the same level in different sections. In other words, they were unsuccessful in *negotiating* a fair exchange of extraordinary investment of resources for extraordinary work performance beyond the confines of their written job descriptions.

View from the Fast Track

The fast-track managers' experiences in these situations were dramatically different from those of their slow-track colleagues. They were seldom surprised by change in programs and procedures—they were among the first to know. In fact, they were often allowed to participate in the discussion of these suggested changes. They described how their bosses bailed them out of problems sometimes at the bosses' expense and how their bosses supported their actions with outsiders. They had learned how to negotiate their roles with their bosses. They also had negotiated some collaboration and co-operation with co-workers outside of their own sections.

What separated these managers into these two distinct groups was their working relationship with their direct superior. The slow-trackers (hired hands), who complained bitterly about their job problems, had relatively ineffective working relationships with their bosses. Because this relationship had not developed into one in which the boss invested and the subordinate provided a return on the investment, the subordinate manager was outside the flow of information and decisions, got little support from the boss, and did not form a competence network. The fast-trackers (trusted assistants), who had effective working relationships, had little to complain about. Of course, they had frustrations on the job, but not with obtaining resources and support from their bosses and co-workers.

We found similar results in a study of 200 bosses and their manager-subordinates in three distinct managerial hierarchies of a government agency. Fast-track trusted assistants did more for their bosses, collaborated more with their bosses on managerial (less structured) duties, and did less routine work than did their slow-track, hired-hand colleagues; further, we found that the bosses and their subordinates had negotiated these collaborations. These negotiations hadn't been formalized in the organization's written documentation, but across hierarchies, it formed part of the organization's unwritten rules. Thus, fast-trackers negotiated exchanges of greater responsibility for greater authority and more resources from their bosses.

Summary

The negotiation process begins with finding an appropriate role through which to outgrow your present job. It then moves to more actively making the role exceed the boundaries of your present job's description. Gradually, this leads to implementing a role that has outgrown the confines of your present job. Eventually, the new role becomes formalized as a promotion, which is the first written acknowledgement of the new role you assume.

An integral part of outgrowing the present job and assuming a new role is the development of an increasingly collaborative relationship with your boss. You gradually negotiate increased responsibilities and assignments for increased authority and resources.

Development and use of resources are discussed more fully in the next chapter.

6

Develop Resources with Bosses and Competent Co-workers

Develop Key Resources: People

Chapter 4 mentioned a key secret of leadership in organizations: To be effective—and on the fast track—in organizations, you must learn how to effectively involve other *people* in helping you to be effective. No matter how competent you are, you need other people if you are to be successful. Chapters 3, 4, and 5 emphasized the importance of your working relationship with your boss: Your boss is your link to the key resources of the organizational hierarchy. Chapters 1 and 2 pointed to an additional resource leading to your success inside your organization: collaborative relationships with competent co-workers. This chapter shows you how to develop and use those resources.

Develop Your Primary Resource: Your Boss

When asked what they have to give to their subordinates, bosses often think in terms of rewards: salary increases, praise, and promotion recommendations. In negative terms, bosses think in terms of withholding rewards, reprimanding, warning, demoting, suspending, or firing an employee. But, as you've seen in the preceding chapters, your boss can offer you far more than these rewards (which usually require formal, written authority from higher levels of the organization). And your boss can impede your career in far more ways than simple punishments (which also require formal, written acknowledgment from higher up).

Some bosses fail to recognize the value of the resources they may have to offer. If so, these resources lay idle—unused by the boss or by the subordinates. When this happens, everyone loses: The subordinates lose the access to resources for developing their careers, the boss loses the opportunity to receive a return on the investment of those resources and the organization loses the potential for increased productivity.

However, when prompted, most bosses recognize the valuable resources they control. They usually also acknowledge that different subordinates gain differential access to these resources. In part, this happens because different subordinates seek access to these resources in varying amounts. But, as shown in previous chapters, some subordinates offer much more return on the boss's investment of these resources.

If you are to successfully outgrow your present job, you must find ways to gain access to your boss's resources, and develop and use those resources to provide a generous return on your boss's investment of those resources.

Obtain Seven Key Resources from Your Boss

The seven key resources to seek, develop, and use are

1. Attention
2. Inside information about the organization
3. Influence in the organization
4. Latitude in performance of your job
5. Access to departmental resources
6. Critical assignments
7. Support

1. Attention. Chapter 3 pointed out 10 career-enhancing activities that required the time and energy—the attention—of your boss.

Chapters 4 and 5 described some of the forms this attention should take if it is to be most advantageous to your career.

Attention of your boss to your work-related needs is critical to your development. You need to know that your boss is monitoring your progress and that your boss will supply the encouragement, leadership, and opportunities to enhance your career. At various times, your boss may need to intervene to help you get back on the right track. At other times, you will need encouragement and a sympathetic ear.

Attention is the key resource through which all of your boss's other resources flow.

2. Information. Information is cherished in organizations, especially inside information, because it affects the ability to make things happen. Information about the future (planning about problems and opportunities, and about visibility upstairs) is especially valuable. Most bosses decide what information to share or not share with which subordinates. A boss may share a lot of information or none at all.

Recall that sharing of information was 1 of the top 10 career-enhancing actions. Bosses can share with their people their working understanding of the hidden face of their companies. This is valuable information because it can make you more effective. Your boss can let you in on the company's special definition of key terms. (For example, in one company, *technoid* meant a person who was excellent at a technical specialty but could not deal with business matters.) These special definitions help fast-track people identify one another. If you are on the fast track, it is assumed that you can speak this inside language appropriately.

In addition, your boss can suggest alternative ways to get things done and the dangers inherent in these ways. These include the identification of troublesome and helpful people and how to deal with them: who you can and cannot trust to do certain things for you. Your boss can tell you about the various competence networks that get things done when they really need to be done. You may even receive advice on how to join these networks and multiply your effectiveness.

The more inside information your boss knows, the more you can learn. With this information, you can avoid mistakes and grow in effectiveness.

3. Influence. Every person in the organization wields some influence—has some impact on the effectiveness of the organization. Each person has access to and uses some of the organization's resources. And each person provides some expertise and some expenditure of energy to do work for the organization. Your boss and you both have this kind of influence within the organization. You also both wield a certain amount of decision-making authority in relation to your work. Even the lowliest of clerks can decide which folders to file first!

Though you each have *some* influence, your boss clearly wields *more* influence, partly because your boss probably has more expertise (including inside information) and has access to more of the company's resources. Most important, your boss possesses far more *decision-making authority* than you do. Your boss has the authority to make crucial decisions affecting your department. Given a set of objectives and responsibilities (determined by those with even greater authority), your boss determines both the priorities for ongoing assignments and special projects and the departmental resources to be allocated to those projects and ongoing work. Further, your boss has the authority to supersede the decisions made by subordinates in the work unit. Finally, your boss can determine *how much* of that authority to share with *which* subordinates.

Your boss is not obliged (by the written rules and policies) to share any of that authority with any subordinates. If your boss does share some authority (above and beyond the written rules), your boss reasonably expects a return of effort and expertise that exceeds the written job description.

Bosses can share their authority with you and other subordinates in a number of different ways. For example, a boss can include your input in decisions for which only the boss is responsible (another of the top 10 ways your boss can enhance your career). Or your boss can allow you to use your boss's name to take actions in prescribed areas. Through negotiation, your boss and you can agree that you will wield some authority in your boss's absence, given that you tell your boss about it at the first opportunity. For example, when your boss is out of town and some expenditure must be made immediately, you could be allowed to make the expenditure for your boss.

Your boss's influence also extends beyond the formal authority of her or his position. For one thing, your boss may also have negotiated to obtain some authority from your boss's boss. Also, your boss has gained some added influence through membership in various competence networks. In rare instances, your boss may agree to let you trade on earned credits in these competence networks.

You must, however, be extremely prudent when trading on your boss's credits in this way. Through this influence, you have the opportunity to make a significant impact both for yourself and for your boss—for good or for ill. And if you diminish your boss's influence, your influence is decreased as well—let alone the effect this would have on your relationship with your boss!

4. Latitude. Closely related to decision-making authority is latitude. Your boss's authority includes monitoring your work performance and superseding your decisions. The more closely your boss monitors your work performance, and the more frequently your boss supersedes your decisions, the less *latitude* you have.

Your boss decides the amount of latitude to grant various subordinates on specific tasks. Some subordinates are required to gain approval at short intervals, others are allowed to go for long periods without reporting to your boss. Even complex tasks can be made trivial by overly specific instructions and short reporting periods.

As you grow out of your job, your boss should increase the latitude in time and scope of assignments to make them progressively more challenging. At first, you must report your progress at relatively short intervals of time. After you have mastered the basics of your present job, you should be given longer reporting intervals. Likewise, the scope of your job should be enlarged progressively as you increase your competence and outgrow your job.

As with your boss's other resources, latitude can be negotiated. Obtain enough latitude to get the work done effectively, but not so much that you lose contact with your boss. Your boss expects you to provide adequate information on your progress. Bosses don't want even pleasant surprises—and certainly not unpleasant ones. However, the greater the latitude you are granted, the harder you must work to keep your boss informed.

5. Access to Departmental Resources. Your boss's boss and your boss have negotiated to determine which of the organization's resources will be made available to your department, as well as how much of each resource. The following resources are among the many your boss may have negotiated to make available to your department:

- Budget for management and supervisory salaries (your boss and any additional supervisory personnel)
- Budget for workers who carry out the actual work of your department (e.g., technicians, operators, assemblers, writers)
- Budget for clerical support (e.g., reception, filing, typing) and for administrative support services (e.g., payroll and benefits, accounts receivable and payable)
- Budget for supplies (office supplies, supplies needed for your department's work, etc.)
- Budget for equipment (computers, furniture, typewriters, phone systems, etc.)
- Allotted office and conference room space
- Budget for, or access to, company transportation vehicles or services
- Budget for training and for professional growth
- Budget for, or access to, information resources (databases, company library, journals, etc.)
- Other budgeted or miscellaneous expenditures

Your boss probably has

- Little or no latitude for negotiating the total amount the organization spends on your department as a whole
- Some latitude on how much of the total is spent on each category of expenditures
- A lot of latitude on who receives or has access to how much of the resources within each category

Thus, you can only negotiate with your boss to gain what your boss has to offer. It is occasionally possible to encourage your boss to try to negotiate for more (as Ray was able to do in the example in Chapter 2). This rarely happens, however, and it would not be worth the risk unless you were sure you could provide your boss with a tremendous advantage for having taken the risk.

Therefore, you must first assess what organizational resources are available to your department, and in what amounts. Next, figure out which of these resources you need in order to outgrow your job. Include both those resources you need in order to do your present job well and those resources you will need in order to take on a new role and tackle challenging assignments.

For each resource that you'd need in your new role, think about what your boss will receive in return for investing that resource in you. For example, if you will need more clerical support to handle your routine tasks, what will you do for your boss and for your department that will *more* than compensate for your use of this resource? If you would like to be freed from your present duties and receive some advanced training, what information and expertise will you return to the people who cover for you while you're gone? How will you make sure your boss and your department benefit from having sponsored you?

Once you have figured out how your boss and your department will profit from having invested their resources in you, you're ready to negotiate for these with your boss. If you make it clear that an investment in you will be more profitable than an investment elsewhere, you're likely to get what you want.

6. Critical Assignments. A primary way of obtaining your department's resources is to use those resources for completing assignments that are critical to your boss's or your department's well-being and to your boss's or your department's work within the organization. You also profit directly from tackling these crucial tasks. Such tasks are opportunities for professional growth and accomplishment, as well as for frustration and failure. Tasks are valued because they're challenging, because they promote visibility upstairs, or because of their side benefits.

Bosses can delegate attractive tasks to all their subordinates, to some and not others, or to no one. Special assignments are a good way of giving you a piece of your boss's job. Through special assignments, you have the opportunity to learn new knowledge and to develop new skills. Special assignments can allow you to grow out of your present job; thus, they form a vital component of your career development.

A natural process that we have witnessed many times in our studies is that of bosses gradually becoming overloaded with work and turning to their subordinates for help. They mention to their subordinates that they have more work than they can possibly do themselves. Some of their subordinates volunteer to go outside of their present jobs and take some of the load off of their bosses as special assignments. Because these special assignments go beyond the written, routine job duties, the boss rewards completion of these assignments by investing one or more of the six other key resources in these subordinates' careers. These special assignments continue to be offered after the work crunch is passed because the boss has discovered that this is a good way to increase the capability of the work unit, and the subordinates have discovered that this leads to outgrowing their present jobs.

Such special assignments can be effective learning opportunities when they are carefully managed. When these assignments are calibrated to your development stage, they become opportunities for successful accomplishment. Challenging tasks can be a most powerful source of work motivation. This collaboration takes time, but it can pay off handsomely.

Your boss can make this natural process even more effective by harnessing its power with the organization's hidden strategies for leadership. Effective managers employ these strategies in their units from the first day. They do not wait for their work to overload them. In fact, conversations with such managers who are planning to take on a new department reveal that they have developed a plan to have some of their people outgrow their jobs and take on specified areas of responsibility. From their first day, they work to implement their plan by selling it to their people. They sell the ideas of finding and using hidden resources, of mutual promotion of careers, and of the employment of special assignments for growth and development. The use of hidden strategies for leadership is described more fully in Part III.

7. Support. If you are to tackle challenging, critical assignments, you must have your boss's support. In addition to providing you with the other six resources, your boss must be willing to share some of the risk involved in these difficult crucial projects. Thus, in high-pressure situations, the degree of support you receive is the extent to which your boss shares some of the heat with you. A boss's support becomes more and more valuable as you accept more challenging assignments. It lessens the risks of performance.

Your boss's support makes special assignments to you feasible. Unless your boss supports your actions with necessary resources to do the work effectively—and backs up your efforts—your acceptance of many special assignments outside of your job would be too risky. This is especially the case for those assignments that require that you stretch yourself and acquire new learning. On such assignments, you are expected to make some mistakes as part of the learning process. Without proper support from your boss, such mistakes may damage your career. With your boss's support, such mistakes should be seen as learning opportunities and not as a sign of incompetence.

To obtain these valuable resources from your boss, you must sell yourself as a wise investment. You need to make it abundantly clear to your boss that an investment in you, more than investments elsewhere, will offer the promise of bountiful profits for your boss —as well as for you.

Seek Out and Join Competence Networks

Thus far, this discussion has focused on your primary resource within the organization: your relationship with your boss. But, as mentioned elsewhere, in order to be truly effective in rising on the fast track, you also need a network of competent co-workers and colleagues.

Appreciating Competence Networks. Competence networks comprise people who get things done and who make ties with other competent people in related units. By tying in with other people who get things done effectively, each competent person can multiply his or her influence throughout the network.

A competence network is not subversive. Competent people simply make the best of the incomplete design of modern organizations.

Networks get things done in ways that could not be anticipated by the designers of modern organizations. Organizations involve human innovations to get things done by coordinating the actions of a number of people. When they work, innovations should be written on paper in order to avoid forgetting how they worked. Unfortunately, there's a lag time between the invention and the written documentation of it. And there's an almost infinite delay between the time an innovation ceases to work and when it's deleted from the written record.

Competence networks develop because competent people are more concerned about getting things done than they are about worshipping the written public-mask documents and procedures of the organization. By inventing new ways of getting things done, competent people help the organization adapt to its changing environment. They do not always succeed, but they are still essential to the continuing health of an organization.

Finding Competent Co-workers and Colleagues. Some of your co-workers are in your work unit and report to your boss, but others are in different departments. Your colleagues may even be in other organizations. They may be suppliers, customers, competitors, shareholders, regulators, or others who share your interest. Developing a network of effective working relationships with co-workers and colleagues can multiply your ability to get things done.

People in competence networks are hard to identify using the public face of the organization. They may hold the department's least responsible position according to the public face—secretary, clerk, administrative assistant, bookkeeper, or the like.

People in competence networks are also hard to recognize by the outward trappings of their offices. They tend not to display signs of their influence. Their workstations might be neat or cluttered, but they seldom contain revealing power symbols.

Joining Competence Networks. You must learn to identify competence, to map the various competence networks, and to join these networks. Unless you acquire expertise in identifying and joining the networks that make the organization work, you will be closed off from them. You must remember that when something needs to be done quickly, only bureaucrats say that it can't be done or that it will take too long. People in competence networks find some way (creatively) to get it done on time and on budget.

Competent workers recognize one another. They don't judge influence based on job titles or the outward trappings of an office. Competent people get things done efficiently and effectively—even things the bureaucrats and the overt public mask of the organization suggest can't be done. After some practice, you can identify competent persons by talking to them on the phone. They speak with confidence about getting things done. They may not know how they're going to do it, but they discover a way through the bureaucratic maze.

Map the competence network carefully. Once you've met a few competent persons, they can help you identify others. When a competent person is needed and cannot be reached immediately, it is better to wait for the competent person than to ask anyone else.

As the competence network becomes evident to you, you must find out how to join it. You can get things done through the competence network without joining it, but to be influential, you must be accepted as a part of it. Joining the network is accomplished through role-making. Through role-making, you get things done for other members of the network in exchange for their getting things done for you—equivalent exchange.

Think of each relationship in the network as if it were a path in a thickly wooded forest. When first finding your way, establishing the path is difficult and takes careful searching. Yet each time the path is traveled, the route becomes clearer and easier to follow. Each trip, you notice new resources or expertise you hadn't observed when you first were so desperate in your search. And each new path leads to other paths. Eventually, almost the entire forest becomes familiar and accessible to you.

Network Building Techniques

Building professional networks is not limited to your immediate job situation; you should begin to build them early in your career and spread them widely. Early network building takes place in school, with your professors and fellow students. Some of these relationships can endure throughout your career. Your job presents multiple opportunities to refine your relationship-building skills. Your boss and your co-workers present your initial challenges. Later, you will have opportunities to expand your network to include relationships with people outside of your company.

Make a special effort to build and maintain your network of relationships. Use methods similar to those described in Chapters 4 and 5, for building effective working relationships with your boss in order to build high-quality relationships with your co-workers and your colleagues.

Role-Finding

Begin by studying your present job situation, which includes those people whom you work with and around: (a) Notice their work-related activities; (b) examine their recent history, with special attention to their successes and failures; (c) evaluate the importance of the various jobs they accomplish; (d) assess their capabilities; (e) determine how you could help them; and (f) consider how they could help you.

Examination of the recent history of these people provides a context for evaluating their present job situations. Get to know them, using the activities described in Chapter 2. Go out of your way to talk to them and show that you are interested in what they have learned. At the appropriate time, offer to help them accomplish their work objectives in whatever ways you can. At all times, be discreet with their information. Let them know that you can be trusted to keep a confidence.

Stories of their successes and failures will suggest who is and is not part of a competence network. Such stories will identify how things were done and who was instrumental in getting various parts accomplished. People who can get things done through hidden strategies will emerge from such stories. Such people are due respect according to their capability regardless of their formal status. If, for example, Nguyen, the unit secretary, can get things done that you cannot, extend to him the respect due his capability.

Role-Making

After you have an understanding of the recent history, concentrate on the present and the future. What do these people do now, and where are they going? You need to evaluate the important parts of their jobs and their capabilities so that you can determine both how you could help them and how they could help you.

Once you have a working understanding of these matters for a particular co-worker or colleague, you can begin courting these relationships, leading them to the negotiation process. Make sure that you have something of value to trade, and don't ask for too much initially. It's better to start small and carefully build the exchange over time. Begin by showing respect, trust, understanding, and sincere interest in your co-workers. Quality relationships take time and care to build. Demonstrate the benefits of a relationship with you; do favors without strings attached. Encourage them to *want* to relate to you; don't pressure them into more of a relationship than they're ready for.

You may find it necessary to modify your interpersonal style somewhat to be more compatible with that of a particular co-worker. For example, Cecilia is assertive and outspoken, so you may have to be boldly candid in describing your offer. However, because Jacob is reserved and careful, you may need to become more tactful and genteel in your approach with him.

After you and your co-worker begin to exchange helping each other, you should be alert to new ways of helping your co-worker. Creatively find ways to offer favors that make an ongoing relationship with you highly rewarding. Too often, such exchanges are one-time events that cease after both fulfill their obligations. Even when both are satisfied with the results, they may not initiate another exchange. You need to be active in finding new ways of helping your co-worker and suggesting how your co-worker could help you. Not until you and your co-worker have exchanged aid with each other several times will the relationship gradually gain some stability. Work toward having the honeymoon lead to a lifelong relationship. Even after you establish the relationship, continue to activate it periodically to maintain it. Otherwise, you may let the weeds grow over the path until it disappears altogether.

Role-Implementing

To build and maintain competence networks requires your scarcest resource—your time—but the payoffs are well worth your investment. Such networks multiply your effectiveness well beyond anything else you might try to do. This multiplying function comes about because your networks allow you to tap into the capabilities of people who can get things done by using your organization's hidden strategies. Often, things that would otherwise be impossible for you to accomplish while working alone can be done with ease when working through your network. In addition, the true value of your network is demonstrated when you really need it to bail you out of a crisis situation.

When you are first starting with a job situation, you must spend a lot of time to develop your networks. However, they offer a route to the fast track. Those who have joined competence networks clearly enjoy a distinct advantage in their ability to get things done in an organization. Those who have not done so may cry that organizational politics caused them to be passed over for a promotion; but they have only themselves to blame for not capitalizing on available competence networks. Effectiveness in organizations requires teamwork, and a most important type of teamwork is found within competence networks. This teamwork often makes the difference between effectiveness and ineffectiveness for an organization.

Also, don't neglect to build networks with people outside of your present company—with your colleagues. As you move up the fast track, you will have increasing opportunities to build collegial relationships with suppliers, customers, competitors, regulators, and other stakeholders. Enthusiastically build such networks; they can multiply your effectiveness beyond the boundaries of your company.

Each pathway in your network will be unique, as each person offers unique insights, expertise, and experience. In turn, you may have different skills, knowledge, and ideas to offer others in your network. Savor the diversity of your contacts within your network, as that diversity offers your network a richness of perspectives and abilities. Not all pathways will be well worn, but even the paths less traveled offer greater breadth and depth of resources to your network as a whole.

Exercise.

Grab a piece of paper, and make a list of all the people in your organization whom you need in order to complete the projects you're assigned. Be sure to include people at all levels of your organization—secretaries, receptionists, janitors, mailroom clerks—anyone who may affect how you perform your job. Add to the list any colleagues outside the organization, who affect your work (suppliers, technicians, delivery personnel). If you already have co-workers with whom you have developed collaborative relationships, ask them to review your list and help you think of additional people you may have omitted.

On another sheet of paper, make a list of all the people in your organization whom you've helped to perform their jobs. Again, really try to think of as many people as possible. Are there people for whom you answer the phone or deliver messages when they're away from their desks? Are there people who need to have your work completed before they can complete their own tasks? Are any other people affected by your projects' quality, timeliness, or use of organizational resources? Ask your trusted co-workers to help you review this list as well. You may want to offer to share your lists with them.

When you first start a job, these lists may be very short; but as you continue in the organization, these lists may grow very long indeed. Use these lists as guide lines for persistently building functional competence networks within your organization.

Summary

Your effectiveness within any organization depends on your ability to involve other people in helping you to perform and to outgrow your job. Your on-the-job capability is enhanced by acquiring seven valuable hidden resources from your boss during the role-making phase of outgrowing your present job:

1. Attention
2. Inside information

3. Influence

4. Latitude

5. Access to departmental resources

6. Critical assignments

7. Support

Methods similar to those described for use with your boss were recommended for building your professional network. In view of the fact that such networks are built, one relationship at a time, the process discussed focused on methods of identifying and making potentially advantageous links. These methods included studying your coworkers in terms of their history of success and failure, their work and their capabilities, and how you could help each other to be more effective. Once you have identified such advantageous relationships, suggestions were offered for negotiating exchanges leading to working relationships that join you to competence networks.

From the outside, this process of earning your way into competence networks is often lumped with a lot of other processes that are not well understood under the label of "company politics." From the inside, in contrast, this process appears quite fair: Those who are willing to do the extra work to build their professional network become more effective and reach the fast track.

Some may protest that no one told them this secret. That protest prompted the writing of this book. Now the information is available—capitalize on it!

7

Solve Problems

Solving a Problem

Geraldo Soto, a senior vice president of a large financial services company, decided that he needed to upgrade his strategies for developing new business. He was not getting his share of new customers, and his profit margins were slipping. He assumed that the problem was that his key salespeople were not making enough calls on prospects. His solution was to request each of his key people to make and document 10 additional calls on new prospects per month. The result? He got his 10 calls per month from each person, but no improvement in new customers or profit margins. The solution was appropriate for the problem he defined, but clearly, he had solved the wrong problem. "What should I do now?" he wondered.

After consulting me and my colleagues, he took his 50 key people off site in two groups, and he engaged them in a three-phased process of problem solving. Together, he and his key people, those involved in the failed calling program, were to (1) unearth their real problem, (2) evaluate a wide variety of solutions to the problem, and (3) investigate alternative ways to implement a solution.

Finding the Problem

Geraldo and his key people spent one full day exploring their business problems to discover a single root problem or set of problems. What emerged was not that employees were making fewer calls, but that their market had changed drastically. Specifically, the problem they identified was that their products and services were targeted at so-called general middle-market businesses, but their market was rapidly becoming differentiated into a number of niches, each demanding specialized products and services. The general middle-market business that remained could now shop for the best margins and play one financial company against the other until they drove down the prices to their liking. Thus, this middle market had become a commodity market in which margins were the main component that made a difference between financial companies. To adapt, new marketing programs were needed.

Active, Open Listening. The process employed to develop this reformulation of the problem was to have Geraldo present his understanding of the situation in detail and for him to ask his salespeople to give him their perspectives. (See Chapter 2 for specifics on using "active listening.") Nothing about this situation was too sensitive to discuss. He was prepared to listen actively to their information and ideas. His salespeople were to decide how to address the situation in relation to several different topics. Once these topics were decided upon by the entire group, each was assigned to be discussed by a small group. Each small group was to discuss the topic and to report back its findings to the entire group.

What Geraldo heard about from his salespeople was the inside information about his salesgroup. He had convinced his salespeople that he wanted to know what was really happening to his group and that he could be trusted to do the right things with their information. He discovered, much to his surprise, that service problems that he thought he had controlled were really only being concealed from him. Moreover, he learned that many of his formerly loyal customers had become shoppers for the best margins because they saw no differences between companies in customer service.

Further, he was appalled to find out that his salespeople felt at a disadvantage in developing new business relative to their competition because they lacked a clear strategy and did not function as a coordinated team. In fact, this was the first time that any of his salespeople, including long-time employees, had had the opportunity to talk about these matters (inside information) with either their colleagues in other departments or their vice president.

Tolerance of Bad News. As a result of this first session—problem finding—Geraldo and his salespeople understood more clearly their strengths and weaknesses relative to their competitors and began to see several new opportunities and threats in new business development. In addition, each department reporting to Geraldo not only became aware of the problems that they had in common with their sister departments but also saw how these common problems affected their particular situation. On this occasion, they had lifted public mask of formal understandings and acknowledged the hidden face of truth.

Neither Geraldo nor his salespeople had done this before, and they were amazed and gratified by the results. Geraldo was surprised by what he was told about what really was happening to his sales division. Although he had suspected some of the things that he was told, he was never confronted with the details in this manner. He was amazed at the way his people capitalized on this opportunity to share their frustrations and hopes with their boss and with their colleagues in other departments.

Geraldo's salespeople had wanted desperately to clear the air and become more effective. This was their chance, and they were not about to let it slip away. In the process, they learned about the problems facing their colleagues, some of which they shared in common and some of which they had unwittingly made worse.

In addition to their stories of failures, they shared stories of their successes. From such stories, they learned what had worked and what had not worked. New ideas were suggested and discussed. They discovered a new appreciation for their common interests and their needs to cooperate in a team effort to solve their common problems.

During these first sessions, Geraldo took notes, which he circulated to all participants a few days later. These notes showed that Geraldo had indeed heard what his salespeople were saying.

Finding a Solution

A second round of problem-solving sessions was held three weeks later. During these sessions, Geraldo and his salespeople agreed to build on the results of the first round by seeking alternative solutions to their identified set of problems: proper market segmentation, development and promotion of new client sources, new product and service development, and market research and advertising. In these sessions, they worked in small groups to discuss and recommend solutions to these problems.

As a result of this second round, each of the seven departments made a commitment to prepare a new business plan. The seven departmental plans were then to be integrated into an overall plan for the entire division. Each department participated in a task force to create the integrated business plan for the division.

Implementing the Solution

The final phase of this process was to find ways to implement the new business plans. As the task force and the departments worked to implement their plans, they sought alternative methods to get the job done. When one method failed to work, they tried another and another until they found one that worked. They knew what they wanted and were prepared to try a number of different ways of achieving their objectives.

A major advantage of this approach appeared during the implementation phase: Because they were all involved in the early search for their problems and had participated in the development of alternative solutions, they understood what they were attempting to achieve and what they wanted to avoid. Moreover, they were all committed to the solution, and they owned the plan. This made changes in the methods of implementation a team effort. When a method was not working, people were willing to try an alternative method. The important thing was to make their plan work and not to remain wedded to a failing method.

These new marketing programs were implemented successfully because those involved in making them work understood and accepted their purposes and procedures. Although it did take longer than the initial autocratic action, it was a more appropriate and better implemented solution to the right problem.

In this chapter, the critical elements for achieving such effective solutions are discussed in terms of the aforementioned three-phased model of problem solving.

Three Phases of Problem Solving

Why Should You Look for Hidden Strategies for Solving Problems?

Bureaucratic managers generally have three good reasons why something unusual cannot be done. Fast-track insider managers somehow find a way to get it done, but don't ask them how—they may not know before it's done. They may need to invent a way to get it done.

Geraldo had initially resisted the suggestion that he involve his key salespeople in building new business programs. He felt that this was his job and that he was accountable to his boss for it. If he involved his key people, somehow his boss would see this as Geraldo's failure. Involving subordinates in managerial problem-solving was foreign to Geraldo's company. Fortunately, Geraldo was desperate and was determined to sell this idea to his boss. The results were so gratifying that Geraldo became the company's champion of this technique.

One key to career success in a modern organization is the ability to effectively solve problems. Good problem solving multiplies your influence far beyond that assumed possible by organizational design.

Some people are amazingly effective at problem solving. Though they don't appear to have any more talent than their peers, they rise more quickly. Their peers don't understand why they're successful, attributing their success to playing politics and favoritism. Politics, perhaps; playing, never. Effective problem-solving stems from a valued set of professional skills.

How Does Each Phase Proceed?

The hidden problem-solving strategy falls into three stages, as shown in Figure 7.1. The three stages are problem finding, solution making,

Figure 7.1 *Three-Stage Process of Creative Problem Solving*

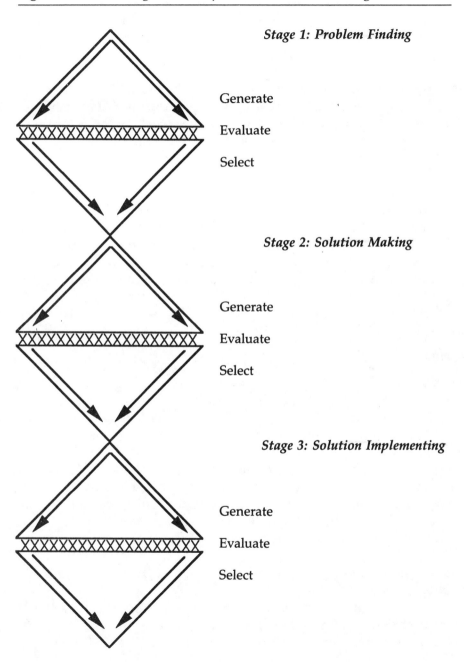

Stage 1: Problem Finding

Generate

Evaluate

Select

Stage 2: Solution Making

Generate

Evaluate

Select

Stage 3: Solution Implementing

Generate

Evaluate

Select

and solution implementing. Within each stage, three processes occur: idea generation, idea evaluation, and idea selection. During the idea-generation process ("brainstorming"), the mind is open to new ways of thinking, new insights into the organization. No idea is considered too implausible, too bizarre, too complex. The result of this process is a set of alternatives.

When the generation process is over, the evaluation process begins. Here, each alternative is tested and combined with other alternatives, using criteria such as relevance, cost, and effectiveness. When there are measurable criteria, evaluation may be time-consuming, but it is seldom difficult. Following evaluation, an optimal alternative is selected.

Thus, as Figure 7.1 shows, each phase goes through three steps: (1) diverging from a single issue to a wide range of possible alternatives, (2) evaluating each of the numerous alternatives against a set of criteria, and (3) narrowing down the alternatives, based on the evaluation, until eventually one or a few alternatives are selected. Ideally, you use this process to find, solve, and resolve potential problems before they materialize. Realistically, you use this to find, solve, and resolve existing problems.

How Does This Work?

Problem-Finding. For Geraldo, he and his salespeople generated a number of alternative formulations of their problems, which ranged from "people are not really trying" to "our markets have changed" and "we need to change to catch up with them." Initially, all alternatives were accepted and noted. Later, once these alternatives were developed through discussion to the status of plausible alternative statements of the problem, they were evaluated against the facts and against each other. In this process, the half a dozen plausible alternatives were pared down to a single formulation of the problem. This alternative was carried forward to the solution-making stage.

Solution-Making. In the solution-making stage, Geraldo and his people generated a long list of things they could do to solve their newly formulated problem. These suggested actions were combined into consistent programs, and these programs were assembled into business plans. Once they were satisfied that they had generated

Exercise. What Are the Three Phases?

1. Finding the Problem. The first step of Phase 1 is to investigate your work situation: Investigate to find any potential problems that you can anticipate or any existing problems that you are experiencing. The way in which you describe a potential or existing problem will also affect the problem-solving process. Think of several ways to state the problem so that you're sure to have included numerous alternatives. That is, you *diverge* from one problematic situation to many alternative descriptive statements of the problem. Next, evaluate each alternative, then select the one that best describes the potential problem. That is, you *converge* from the many possible alternatives to select the one (or few) alternative(s) that you evaluated as being best.

2. Finding the Solution. In Phase 2, brainstorm a number of alternative solutions (diverge) to the potential problem you identified. Be wildly creative in coming up with these. What seems at first like an offbeat solution may either end up being the best one or lead you to find the best one. Next, evaluate each solution, taking the time to explore the relative costs and benefits of each alternative. When considering costs, be sure to include time and energy, as well as other resources. When considering benefits, consider intangibles such as fostering good will and mutual respect among those who will participate in the process or who will be affected by the outcome. Once you've carefully considered the alternatives, choose the one (converge) that offers the best outcome at the least cost to you and your department.

3. Finding the Suitable Implementation. In Phase 3, think of several ways (diverge) to implement the solutions you selected. As with the other phases, evaluate each alternative carefully, and then choose (converge) the best one (that is, the one that offers the best outcome at the least cost). This does *not* end the process, however. The next step may be the most difficult one: Implement the solution in the way you have chosen.

most of the feasible solutions, they began to evaluate them, using cost-effectiveness and risk criteria. This evaluation produced a set of coordinated business plans directed at recapturing their market share and improving their profitability.

Solution-Implementing. These business plans were carried forward to the solution-implementing stage. In this stage, they generated alternative ways of putting their plans into effect. They studied their markets by gathering information from their current and prospective customers, various market experts, their colleagues in other departments, and even their competitors. Once a number of alternative implementation plans were refined, they evaluated them in terms of their likelihood of being put into effect properly and maintained over time.

Nonsequential Exceptions. The three stages do not always occur in the sequence shown in Figure 7.1. Problems discovered in the second or third stage may send the process back to the first stage. It is not uncommon to find yourself implementing a solution to the wrong problem. When this happens, the process should return to stage one. This adaptability may appear inefficient, but it reduces the chances of solving the wrong problem.

Zero In or Zero Out. Perhaps the greatest threat to the problem-solving process is losing sight of the main objective, which is to implement a solution that effectively solves the root problem. This objective must be emphasized throughout the process. No matter how elegant the solution appears, it must deal with the problem, or it is worthless.

How Can You Find the Problem?

Patient Pursuit of the Problem. Geraldo had initially formulated his problem as how he could get his lending officers to make more business development calls. He had reasoned that at least 10% of such calls would successfully lead to new business. Thus, more calls would translate into more business. Though his reasoning was logical, as was his solution, he solved the wrong problem. The problem was how to achieve more higher-margin business.

As humans, we tend to accept quickly our first approximation of a statement of a problem. To overcome this natural impulse, we must consciously work at problem finding. In this stage, you ask yourself what the symptoms or disturbing events are and what is producing them.

Do we have a real problem or merely an apparent one? For example, it is not uncommon for productivity to decline for a period of time without being a real problem. This can happen as a normal fluctuation in the business cycle. If we take no action, productivity may rebound. Similarly, our costs can increase or decrease for periods of time without signaling any real problem. This does not suggest that you not study the situation, but only that you do not overreact. Concluding that you do not have a real problem is not a waste of time.

Problem-finding tasks range from seeking refinements in small operational systems to diagnosing chronic dysfunctions in major systems. This requires not only technical and managerial expertise, but also techniques for developing both a tolerance of ambiguity and a deferral of judgment.

Tolerance of Ambiguity. Tolerance of ambiguity allows you to live with uncertainty by actively considering multiple feasible explanations (which often conflict with one another) at the same time. The greater your tolerance of ambiguity, the longer you can resist the need to find a quick solution.

Intolerance of ambiguity is rooted deep in the human psyche. Science and technology couldn't exist without the amazing human urge to search for underlying patterns in whatever seems ambiguous and confusing. Uncertainty and chaos make us feel uneasy and prompt us to look for orderly patterns within the disorder. However, in our haste to find a quick answer, we occasionally misidentify patterns (such as the long-held belief that the sun revolves around the earth). Or we identify patterns that don't exist. (Have you ever been told that your behavior was typical of people with your astrological sign?)

When making decisions, this tendency to seek patterns causes us to relate new problems (unintelligible chaos) to familiar problems (understandable patterns). In many ways, this helps to make the otherwise bewildering and intimidating problem more understandable and solvable. We quickly see a pattern within the problem, as we had already identified the pattern in the familiar problem.

If the underlying cause of the new problem is indeed related to the source of the familiar problem, and the solution to the familiar problem can be applied to the new problem, we've quickly found a solution to the new problem. Thus, in some situations, this strategy works.

Unfortunately, this strategy does not work for many problems, especially for complex ones. Not realizing this, we tend to overgeneralize and oversimplify complex new problems, relating them to familiar problems that really don't share a common underlying pattern. We quickly choose a simple, familiar, obvious answer instead of a complex, innovative, subtle one. When we superimpose the familiar problem's solution onto the novel problem, it doesn't work.

For example, when Geraldo saw profit margins slipping, he overgeneralized a familiar problem (low profit margin because salespeople aren't contacting enough prospects to generate sales) to the new problem (decreasing profit margins due to market changes). One way to contend with our impatience to eliminate ambiguity is to deliberately postpone making decisions until we have had time to explore all the alternatives.

Deferral of Judgment. People with problems feel intense pressure, imposed by themselves and by others, to quickly conclude the problem-finding phase of problem solving. They jump to conclusions about the nature of the problem instead of deferring judgment until they can invest enough time to find the true problem. They then spend much more time on choosing a solution and implementing the solution. This sometimes leads to very thoroughly and effectively solving the *wrong* problem. Often, entire departments are reorganized or procedures redesigned every year or so without getting at the real problem. Even the most creative solution to the wrong problem is wasteful.

Deferring judgment until all the alternatives are considered helps to alleviate the pressure to dismiss alternative questions and answers prematurely. The three-step technique for deferring judgment (idea generation, idea evaluation, and idea selection) encourages more thoughtful consideration of novel alternatives. Once novel alternatives are examined more carefully, they become increasingly familiar, and you can evaluate them more realistically. In order to generate new ideas, you study all the available information, even generating new information in some cases. Take the time to explore alternative explanations.

American versus Japanese Approaches. For American managers, this tendency to leap to familiar conclusions can be exacerbated by their on-the-job training. They're trained to make hard-and-fast evalua-

---

Exercise.

Think about your current work situation. In your career notebook, jot down some common problems you've faced more than once in your work situation. After each problem, write down what you now see as causing the problem. Next, begin generating ideas (Step 1 of the three-step process) to see if there are other factors that contribute to your problem. Ask your trusted co-workers for help in coming up with ideas you might have overlooked. Defer your judgment (Steps 2 and 3, evaluation and selection) until you've really explored fully all the possible ideas.

When you use the three-step approach, you can better understand your situation. Don't settle for inferior but clear-cut questions and answers when more accurate ones are available, given a bit more searching. Generate new alternatives. Once you and your problem-solving team have formulated a wide array of alternatives, you can evaluate them and begin to narrow them down in order to select the best one (or a few). You may find that the newly familiar alternatives lead to more promising possibilities.

Repeat this three-step process for each common problem you noted. Did your new answers surprise you? If so, you may need to solve future problems by consciously going through each of these three steps until you have incorporated it into your personal method for solving problems. Once you're completely immersed in the three-phase, three-step process, you'll naturally use it to solve all the problems you encounter.

tions and to trust their gut reactions to situations. This training often leads them to reject many alternatives before they fully understand the implications of each. They may habitually reject an alternative simply because it is new. They distrust the unknown, the untried, and the unfamiliar; they quickly embrace conventional explanations.

In Japan, on the other hand, managers spend most of their time and energy on finding and defining the problem. When finding the problem, the Japanese seek consensus among all the people who will be involved in implementing the solution. By involving many people in formulating the problem, they overcome some of the pressure for a quick-and-dirty statement of the problem.

When my colleagues and I trained professional design engineers who worked for a large manufacturing company to use the three-phase (finding a problem, a solution, and an implementation), three-step (idea generation, evaluation, selection) technique, they became much more effective in solving problems they encountered than their colleagues who didn't receive this training. Furthermore, they appreciated the value of this strategy when they used it to solve real problems on their jobs.

We also studied the traditional American strategy of management in which the manager alone determines how to solve the problem. We compared it with the Japanese strategy of management by consensus (by everyone who will be involved in the implementation). For most situations, the Japanese strategy of management by consensus works more effectively than the American solitary-manager strategy.

In some situations, however, total consensus management works less effectively. For highly technical matters, consensus management involves too many people who don't understand key technical features of the problem. Also, with some critical problems, a decision must be reached quickly. If so, involve as many of the key people as possible, but not so many that agreement can't be reached as quickly as it's needed.

Nonetheless, as much as possible, avoid having a manager sit alone in an office and make a decision that others must implement. The decision made from the perspective of only one person is likely to be less effective for solving the problem. Further, without participation in making the decision, workers feel less committed to implementing it effectively.

Criteria for Effectively Solving a Problem

Two Components of Decision Quality: Technical Quality and Implementability. Both components must be adequate. A technically outstanding decision that is poorly implemented is a waste, as is the reverse. To ensure that implementability is emphasized, involve those who will be critical to implementation in every phase of the decision.

Jacqueline Couzine, an accounting analyst for a large department store chain, designed a technically ingenious cost control system. Though her system worked well on the computer, after six months of effort, she still could not get the store clerks to implement it properly. Sales employees continually entered faulty data into Jacqueline's system.

Postmortem study of this failure revealed that her system made unrealistic demands on salespeople. Once she had this information and involved the sales employees, she was able to redesign the system and implement it effectively.

Jacqueline had made the mistake of not involving those people who would be critical to implementing her system. She failed to expand her problem to include ways to implement her new system. Salespeople had seen the need to input point-of-sale data into Jacqueline's system as a threat to their job security. They didn't understand how this system would improve their situation. Once the salespeople and Jacqueline discussed the implications for them, and Jacqueline answered their questions, the program received the needed cooperation.

Strengths and Weaknesses. During the problem-finding phase, Geraldo's problem-solving team uncovered their strengths, such as the competence and commitment of their people; their contacts in every corner of their financial markets; and a CEO who was looking to improve corporate performance. They also exposed their own weaknesses: failure to innovate new products, services, and marketing programs to stay on top of their changing markets; and a lack of teamwork among people in different departments. Moreover, their discussions revealed a large number of opportunities that could be exploited. Once they had found their problem, they knew where they wanted to go. Next, they needed to decide how they should get there.

How Can You Find the Solution?

For Geraldo's team, finding the solution began with their statement of the problem: How can we improve our high-margin business without unduly increasing our risks? From this flowed a number of related questions:

- What products and services will new customers see as value added?
- How do we reach these new customers?
- How do we deliver what these customers seek better than our competitors?
- How do we ensure that we stay close to our customers over time?

A number of alternatives were generated for each question. Once the options were identified, they were evaluated in terms of their cost-effectiveness, technical quality, and implementability. After reviewing these evaluations, they selected the optimal alternative features from each business plan. From this, they formulated an integrated overall business plan for how they would achieve their objectives.

The plan for action must deal, not just with each individual department's system, but also with all the related systems. Systems are connected; a change in one causes changes throughout. Side effects cannot always be foreseen, but a serious effort should be made to do so. Although they attempted to anticipate some of the problems that they would face during implementation, they recognized that effective implementations would have to be selected in a separate phase, once they got close to putting their plans into action.

Their business plans called for a new marketing function in the division, geared to keeping track of their markets and coordinating new business development activities among all departments. In addition, each department in the division had its own new business plan, which was targeted at its own markets and coordinated with the other departments. Thus, the two identified weaknesses were addressed by the overall and the individual business plans.

Finding the solution uses the products of the problem-finding process—various formulations of the questions to be answered. The expertise acquired during problem-solving tasks should be used to anticipate implementation problems, including side effects, and to begin contingency planning. Anticipate implementation problems to ensure effective action in the solution-finding process.

Anticipate Problems. Contingency planning is designed to minimize threats and to capitalize on opportunities. Though the particulars of the plan must be left open and slowly filled in, the general form of the plan can be developed. Without contingency planning, good decisions are harder to make in the "heat of battle." Under pressure, we tend to resort to the habitual; we become reactive rather than proactive. New learning is difficult if not impossible during the event. There is no time to consider all the threats and opportunities.

Finding the solution begins with the alternative formulations of the problem (developed in the problem-finding phase), continues with the generation of alternative solutions (diverging), proceeds with the evaluations of the solutions, and finishes up with selecting the alternative evaluated as optimal (converging). The diverging process here is like the diverging process in the problem-finding phase: tolerate ambiguity and defer judgment. Again, the objective is to generate many alternatives and to actively consider these alternatives for a while.

Solution Evaluation. After the generating process is over, and the alternatives have been allowed to simmer for a while the evaluation phase begins.

The evaluation phase has received the most attention from decision-making technologists. Many methods are available to assist in the process. These methods are taught in the professional schools and in management development and training programs in industry. They are so pervasive, in fact, that many people think that the evaluation of solutions is all there is to problem solving.

Formal training in problem solving focuses on the evaluation of alternatives and on analytical tools. This approach can lead to unfortunate outcomes for the organization. Engineers and managers may unwittingly apply their analytical tools to problems that have been crudely formulated and inadequately explored for alternatives. The tools work very well, but they can't produce a silk purse from a sow's ear.

Choose Economy. Competing themes can sometimes dominate problem-solving. For example, choosing to use only cutting-edge technology may impede selection of the optimal solution. Cutting-edge technology may include the latest hardware (computers, robots, satellites), or the most popular (faddish) software (management systems and procedures). Cutting-edge technology can be a source of pride, but it sometimes leads to ineffective action. Effective action seeks only the least expensive and lowest level of current hardware and software that will get the job done. This economy should also be applied to other aspects of the solution. Generally, if two solutions are otherwise equally effective, prefer the solution that causes the least disruption of ongoing functions and procedures or that requires the smallest amount of extra time and energy for implementation. Effective action calls for programs that cost the least from the organization's resources and that produce the minimum of disruption in ongoing systems while still getting the job done.

Solution Selection. Another pitfall at this step is to overanalyze alternatives. There is always one more analytical technique to try and one more data base to check. You can get trapped into the joys of analysis and lose sight of your objective. Remember this rule from Chapter 1: Never make a decision until you must, but be prepared to make it at a moment's notice. Clearly, deadlines must be set to limit the time devoted to this step.

For Geraldo and his salespeople, they finally came to a consensus regarding their solution. They understood that these plans were subject to change; to be tested and refined until they achieved their objective or were dropped. The next step was to sell their solution to the CEO. Geraldo used the negotiation strategies described in Chapters 4, 5, and 6 to convince the CEO of the merit of their solution.

How Can You Implement the Solution?

Using the Networks. Geraldo's CEO approved the plan, pending support from the other division heads. Thus, Geraldo and his salespeople began the solution-implementing phase by asking the key people involved in each action program to assure their contributions. Many of these key people were in different divisions and had little knowledge or interest in the new business plans of Geraldo's division. Geraldo's team discussed these questions, and they generated alternatives. They suggested a number of different new ways of involving the key people in the other divisions. They also discovered that some of their people had effective working relationships with key people in other divisions, which could prove invaluable.

Evaluation of these alternatives produced both a better understanding of the competence networks in the company and a better set of plans to capitalize on these networks, in order to effectively implement the new business programs. Those of Geraldo's people who had good contacts were charged with important assignments that utilized these contacts. (Notice how they profit from their competence networks.) In terms of implementation, key people in distant departments who did not have an effective contact in Geraldo's division were to be recruited and sold on the program. Senior management was sold on the program through a series of presentations and discussions.

Champions. Geraldo was the overall champion, and his marketing representative within each department served as a champion in that department's program. As champions, their role was to make the program work in spite of any obstacles. They were to be cheerleaders and team players, maintaining their enthusiasm for the program long after the novelty had worn off. In short, their driving force was to make this new business development program effective.

Making Implementation Work

Monitoring and Adaptation. The solution-making phase produces an action program, including contingency plans and implementation procedures. After that, the implementation process begins. This process requires the commitment of people who assisted in the problem-finding and solution-making phases. No matter how thorough the planning process, people still need to implement the action program, taking the proper actions at the proper times. Creative managers do not assume they can anticipate every contingency that may occur. They recognize that the process must be monitored throughout the implementation phase.

Action plans must be tested and refined through actual operation. Simplifying assumptions made during the planning process may need to be changed. The main thrust of the implementation phase is to make the program operational in a particular situation, with the available resources (human, material, and financial).

Pride of ownership in an action plan cannot be jealously guarded, as it only lowers the chances for successful implementation. Involving others in adapting a plan to a particular situation is the only way to make it feasible.

Trade-Offs. Championing a concept involves a series of trade-offs. One trade-off is between (a) preserving the essential features of the program and (b) encouraging necessary modifications for effective implementation. Crucial to this is understanding which features are essential and which are not. Modifications should be negotiated with the others involved in implementation.

Another trade-off is between (a) involving everyone who wants to be involved and (b) involving only those who understand the technical requirements of the program. The former may result in the blind leading the sighted, causing the program to lose its main thrust. The latter preserves the main thrust of the program but at the expense of commitment and enthusiasm.

The implementation process consists of the now-familiar three steps: diverge to generate alternatives, evaluate the numerous possibilities, and subsequently converge to select favored procedures. Again, tolerate ambiguity and defer judgment in order to discover new alternatives. The more people involved in the divergent generating of ideas, the harder it is to prevent premature rejection of novel alternatives.

Refinements. Once a program is implemented, it must be tested and refined periodically to keep it current. When an action program is no longer effective, it should be replaced. However, programs tend to become functionally autonomous and survive much longer than they should. It often takes as much energy to discontinue an ineffective program as it does to develop an effective one. Knowing when and how to discontinue an ineffective program is an important skill.

When Should the Three-Phase Strategy Be Used?

Although we have explored the various phases of the problem-solving process rather slowly, it unfolds quite rapidly when in use. Once you master it, you'll find that it doesn't take much longer than the traditional problem-solving process. For simple or relatively easy problems, the complete process is not required, although the problem-finding phase should always be employed to determine whether the traditional or three-phase, three-step process should be used.

Adaptability to change is a key characteristic of effective management. Perhaps, the greatest threat to adaptability are the hidden assumptions that we make. Without knowing it, we often restrict our decision alternatives. To make better decisions, we must admit our biases and overcome them. Three-phase problem solving and other hidden strategies provide valuable tools in our endeavor to successfully be the best we can be.

Using the Three-Phase Technique on Hidden Problems

Result of the Problem

Art Brewer, the plant manager of a major division of a large auto parts manufacturing corporation, complained that his management team was not adapting to meet stronger demands for their plant's products. They had reached the limits of their productive capacity and needed to expand. However, Art's team resisted putting together a strategic plan to move them to their larger capacity.

Art found that he was forced to make all of the decisions. Although he delegated authority to make decisions about various aspects of the plan, his subordinates would wait until Art made the decision for them. Of course, Art could not do both his own and his staff's work. He was burning out. He was always tired, frequently complained of headaches, and talked about his frustrations with any peer who would listen.

"Why won't my people do their jobs and help me plan this expansion?" he asked.

Finding the Problem

Art hired Michelle Woodward, a new staff assistant to help develop the expansion plan. Michelle began the process of understanding the hidden problem by talking to Art, Art's staff, other division managers, and some long-time employees on the shop floor. Michelle wanted to understand why Art was left alone to put the expansion plan together.

Authority. Michelle discovered that Art's staff really did not wield any authority. Although their job descriptions stated that they had authority in specified areas, Art's actions denied these statements. Their previous attempts to exercise decision-making authority were frustrated by Art. Sometimes he would override their decisions. Other times, he would authorize others to make their decisions. Consequently, decision-making authority really was not being delegated. The public mask stated that they possessed the necessary authority, but the hidden strategies denied it.

Expertise. Michelle also discovered that Art's staff did not have the expertise necessary to prepare an expansion plan. They were competent to manage the ongoing process, but they could not propose an expanded organization. Many of the staff managers had been promoted from the shop floor without the specified training for each promotion.

Finding the Solution

Training. Michelle proposed, and Art accepted a program to train Art and his staff in both (a) management processes, including the delegation of decision-making authority with accountability, and (b) capacity expansion planning. They were to do this while undertaking the actual planning process.

Implementing the Solution

This learning and doing project was a good strategic management program for Art and his staff. Over a six-month period, they acquired the knowledge and skills needed to (a) prepare the expansion plan and (b) begin the process of developing Art's team. Michelle also learned a good deal about the organization's hidden aspects of its big picture, which will serve her well with the company.

Where the demands of the markets are felt, the need for hidden strategies emerges. When Art could not cope with his plant's undercapacity any longer, he was forced to question his assumptions based on the written rules and conventional strategies. Without this pressure, Michelle would not have been permitted to reveal that these assumptions were erroneous. Such pressures open windows for change. The trick is to be in a position to influence action when these windows are open.

Rewards of Problem Solving

Both Michelle and Geraldo derived several benefits of solving their problems, beyond the immediate satisfaction of having solved the problem:

- *Increased insider information*: Both Geraldo and Michelle found out a great deal about how their organizations work, who knows whom in their organizations, and how things get done in their organizations.

- *Increased credibility and influence*: Geraldo and Michelle increased each one, not only within their own work units, but also throughout other divisions in their organizations.

- *Widened networks*: They both clearly added many new connections and working relationships to their competence networks.

- *Increased skills*: They both learned a lot from their experiences—what *didn't* work, as well as what did—and are both much more expertly prepared to solve the next problems they encounter.

Summary

This chapter described the hidden three-phase process of problem solving. Tolerance for ambiguity and deferral of judgment skills are required for all three stages. The first stage, *problem finding*, formulates the problem, trying to avoid solving the wrong problem. The second stage, *solution finding*, looks for an appropriate solution to the problem. The third stage, *solution implementing*, tries to make the solution work.

Each of the stages includes three steps: (1) generate numerous possibilities, (2) evaluate them, then (3) select the best one. Because these three steps are repeated throughout each phase of the process, this process is called "recursive." If, at any point in the process, things don't seem to be working well, you can repeat these three steps in order to find and remove the obstacle blocking the path of the process. In fact, most problems are actually solved by frequently re-exploring one or more phases of this process until a satisfactory solution is reached.

All three stages and all three steps within each stage are necessary to effectively solve the right problem. Too little care given to any of these results in ineffective problem solving.

In Part III, these problem-solving techniques are applied to fast-track leadership strategies.

III

Savoring Success: Practicing Fast-Track Leadership

Lead Others to the Fast Track

Part I of this book told you how to discover the unwritten rules of your organization; Part II explained how to apply those rules through hidden strategies, in order to manage your career. Throughout both parts, the secrets for developing your career on the fast track to success involved your figuring out how to effectively tap the resources of your organization and use them to accomplish important work for the organization. Parts I and II told you how to attain leadership. Part III tells you how to demonstrate leadership.

As you become an insider within the organization, you are asked to lead others to do the same. Once you've learned the unwritten rules and mastered the hidden strategies, you're ready to guide others to manage their own careers.

Develop the Full Breadth of Talent Available

Clearly, as a leader, you must find and develop the talents of the people whom you lead. Many talented people, however, have never had a chance to develop their talents, to discover the secrets of how organizations work, to realize their potential for success. For many years, American organizations allowed irrational biases to determine who would or wouldn't become an insider. Paternalism, racism, sexism, cronyism, and nepotism kept "old boy" networks flourishing and excluded "outsiders" from their ranks. For decades, American organizations underemployed, undervalued, and underutilized any potential fast-trackers who looked or behaved differently from the already entrenched "insiders." Hence, these "outsiders" have been limited in their ability to develop and use their potential expertise and leadership.

Many organizations have been forced to see that their narrow view of self-interest has been their undoing. Their ironclad procedures are rusting, and their petrified rules are crumbling. Their narrow "isms" excluded too many of the potential fast-trackers who might otherwise have helped these organizations to adapt and compete in the world market. Don't permit wasteful squandering of the diverse talents within your organization. Begin now to discover the hidden potential talents and expertise of all the people whom you lead.

Start Now

There can be no *wrong* time for advancing your career and the careers of those whom you lead. Whenever you decide to move along the fast track and to help others to do so, you and they will profit from doing so. However, doing so right now is particularly advantageous. Ever-increasing changes in the international marketplace are causing U.S. organizations to need urgently the competitive edge that fast-trackers offer. As an insider, a leader within your organization, you can show others the way to the fast track. You, your organization, and those you lead will benefit.

Lead the Leaders

Part III comprises four chapters that can increase your expertise as a leader within your organization. Chapter 8 briefly describes what happens when an organization doesn't have effective strategies for coping in dynamic situations. The chapter then explains a plan for gathering and disseminating inside information in order to manage and control the rapid changes the organization confronts. The plan emphasizes communication of needs within the primary working relationship—the relationship between a superior and a subordinate.

Chapter 9 more fully describes this primary relationship, elaborating some of the ideas from Part II, but doing so from the perspective of the supervisor instead of the subordinate. Chapter 10 describes ways of integrating the many diverse perspectives that coexist within an organization. And Chapter 11 describes how to teach others what you've learned about the unwritten rules and hidden strategies of organizations. Lead other *potential* leaders to the fast track.

8

How Leaders Can Find Inside Information

The Need for Fast-Track Leaders

The introduction to Part III described how U.S. organizations are responding to radical changes in technology, in international competition, and in the marketplace: with some notable exceptions, miserably. They desperately need insiders who can quickly master existing projects and pursue new ones enthusiastically, who eagerly tackle novel and unexpected challenges. Organizations cry out for achievers who can immediately enhance organizations' well-being by quickly grasping how things really work, identifying who can get things done, and applying that information to make their part of the organization perform superbly.

Fast-track insiders can make their organizations perform more effectively because they have mastered the complexities of today's business, surmounted its obstacles, and cut through its ambiguities to find the secrets of making their organizations perform well. They have penetrated the veneer of written documents and conventional routines and procedures, and they've uncovered the inside information on the way things really get done in organizations.

As the degree and number of changes in our lives multiply at an alarming rate, standard routines and customary procedures become decreasingly useful. We need ever-greater numbers of insiders who

159

can find or develop ways of adapting to and profiting from change. Not only are you needed as a fast-tracker, but you are also needed as a leader, to guide others onto the fast track and to help your organization to grow and prosper in a context of accelerating change.

This chapter shows a situation in which an entire management hierarchy of more than 100 positions underwent a process designed to respond to changes occurring in the marketplace. The process was intended to (1) update the hierarchy's written documentation, (2) reveal major features of the unwritten rules and hidden strategies to both managers and their superiors, and (3) encourage leaders to use and promote these strategies at all levels of the organization.

The Problem

Fragmentation and Inflexible Response to Change

The CEO of a medium-sized company complained that his organization, which had doubled its size in the previous five years, was becoming unresponsive to his directions. Although the company's markets were becoming more volatile, the organization was becoming less flexible and adaptable.

"What has gone wrong with my plan?" he asked. "Are we suffering the pains of our success? How can we get back on track?"

The leadership of the company had become compartmentalized. All the managers viewed their functions as independent and were moving in uncoordinated directions. Even superiors and their immediate subordinates had trouble seeing eye to eye. As a by-product of its tremendous growth, the organization had become too fragmented. The problem was to reverse this disorganizing process and build a basic agreement between superiors and their subordinates and among peers.

One of the first casualties of this rapid growth was written documentation. Each department had reacted to new challenges and new threats by changing its objectives and procedures. Jobs and families of jobs were changed informally in response to the changing demands of growth. New responsibilities were added, and some established responsibilities were deleted. Some managers were doing things without the proper authority, and others were holding back from taking proper action because they were uncertain of their authority. In sum, written documentation was completely outdated—it described a smaller and less complicated organization.

Clearly, this organization had outgrown its existing conventions and documents, and needed to create new ones that would fit its new dimensions. Moreover, the unwritten rules and hidden strategies of the organization had scattered in too many divergent directions. Management needed to focus on their shared organizational objectives and to rationalize their strategies in pursuing those objectives.

Finding the Problem

Though the CEO knew something had gone wrong with his plan, he really didn't know what the problem was or how to solve it. He asked me and my colleagues to help him. Our first step in helping to solve the problem was to find the problem. (For more information on three-phased problem solving, refer to Chapter 7.) Before trying to find the macrocosmic problem of the entire organization, we decided to examine the basic working relationship of the organization: the relationship between supervisor and subordinate.

Job Descriptions

To understand the working relationships between subordinates and supervisors, we explored five basic questions:

1. What do supervisors need from their subordinates in order to do their jobs?
2. What do subordinates need from their supervisors in order to do their jobs?
3. What are each person's job responsibilities?
4. What are the priorities for what should be done, and what actually gets done in this working relationship?
5. How do things get done when new situations arise?

   If supervisors and subordinates disagreed on these fundamental issues, we'd gain insight into why the organization was faltering in its mission.

These five questions go beyond the typical job description queries that ask people to describe what they do on their jobs. The third question, about job responsibilities, comes the closest, but it isn't the same. Job responsibilities relate to the obligations a worker is charged to fulfill rather than the duties a worker is expected to perform. How those obligations are fulfilled is not addressed by Question 3.

Questions 1, 2, 4, and 5 move the focus of attention from the job itself to the working relationship between the subordinate and the supervisor. As Parts I and II showed, this relationship usually provides the key to reaching the fast track. As a subordinate, your relationship to your supervisor may determine how easily and quickly you ride on the fast track. As a supervisor, your relationship to your subordinates may either help or hinder their progress toward the fast track.

To illustrate this problem-finding process, we look at three employees. Their working relationships show some of the hidden aspects of the organization that needed to be revealed and understood in order to find the problem. Kikanza Washington is the head of the research and development department, and Warren Agajeenian is a valuable manager within her department. Cindy Pfeiffer is a relatively new technician who reports directly to Warren.

1. What do supervisors need from their subordinates in order to do their jobs? This first question concerns *accountability*. To be sure that Warren is doing what Kikanza needs in order to do her job, she needs a way of ensuring that Warren is accountable to her for doing those things. To ensure Warren's accountability, Kikanza asks Warren to inform her adequately about his progress on various projects. In this way, she can be confident that the projects are proceeding as they should.

From Kikanza's viewpoint, pleasant surprises don't exist; supervisors expect to be informed about what is happening in their units. Likewise, Warren expects accountability from Cindy, and he expects Cindy to keep him informed. Both supervisors are expected by *their* supervisors to know what's happening in their units, so they expect their subordinates to make sure they know.

Both the supervisor and the subordinate are responsible for seeing to it that this question is answered adequately. Many people in both roles fail to ask this question frequently enough. It's easy to get caught up in coping with the present work and neglect to seek (or to supply) the information that superiors need from their subordinates.

This neglect can have negative repercussions up and down the management hierarchy. At Kikanza's level, she expects Warren and her other subordinates to keep her informed of everything that goes on in his unit. Similarly, Warren expects Cindy and his other subordinates to keep him informed. Occasionally, Kikanza is surprised by something (good or bad) that's going on in Warren's unit. If she hears of it from a peer or from *her* superior, she feels disconcerted at best. It implies that she's not doing her job effectively.

For example, on one occasion, the manager of the publications department asked her, "What happened to your schedule? I thought we weren't going to have your proposal for the circuit-board project until July." Kikanza had been unaware that the proposal's schedule had been advanced. She was embarrassed that she hadn't already known of the schedule change, and she was angry that Warren hadn't met his obligation to keep her informed and to be accountable to her about what goes on in his work unit.

In this instance, Warren hadn't informed Kikanza because he hadn't been informed by Cindy, who was developing and testing the circuit-board prototype for the proposal. Warren had been flustered that he appeared not to be doing his job effectively. The effect on Cindy and Warren's working relationship was not positive, to say the least.

2. What do subordinates need from their supervisors in order to do their jobs? This second question concerns the resources that the subordinate needs from the superior:

• Access to departmental resources
• Attention
• Latitude in performance of the job
• Support
• Influence and authority in the organization
• Inside information about the organization

These resources (and a seventh resource, needed for outgrowing the present job—critical assignments) were discussed more fully in Chapter 6. However, two of these resources deserve extra attention here, as disagreements about these bore directly on the problem we were searching for: the inside information that the supervisor makes available to the subordinate, and the authority that the supervisor delegates to the subordinate.

The need for *inside information* goes up and down the hierarchy. Just as Kikanza needs to stay informed about Warren's projects, and Warren about Cindy's, both Warren and Cindy need to be informed about any inside information that might help them in performing their own jobs. Warren needs to know about anything relevant that happens in other sections of the research and development department and in other departments in the organization. Cindy needs to know about anything relevant that happens in Warren's work unit.

For example, Kikanza had heard from a friend in accounting that this quarter's profits were down, so there was some noise about freezing any capital expenditures for a while. Foreseeing possible cuts or freezes in her equipment expenditures, Kikanza immediately told Warren so that he could purchase some testing equipment that he had planned to purchase for an incoming project.

Because Warren had been forewarned, he was able to buy the equipment, essential to the final stages of the project. If Kikanza hadn't advised him, he might have waited until the need for the equipment was more imminent—and the organization was in the middle of a spending freeze on equipment purchases. Likewise, Warren lets Cindy know of any procedures or techniques used in other work units that might help Cindy in her work.

Assumptions regarding *authority* can also help or hinder an organization. When subordinates and superiors disagree about authority, one of five outcomes may occur:

1. Only one of the parties takes appropriate action
2. One of the parties takes inappropriate action
3. Both parties act independently
4. Neither acts, but both assume that the other acted
5. Neither acts, but only one party sees the need for action

When only one of the parties takes action and, fortuitously, the action taken is appropriate, all goes well. However, if the action was inappropriate, the question of authority may injure the working relationship. The other three possibilities also have unfortunate consequences. If both parties act independently, they may trip over each other, cancel out each other's efforts, or simply duplicate efforts. With the last two outcomes, the appropriate action remains unexecuted.

For example, Cindy assumed that she was authorized to write a draft of the proposal for the circuit-board project because she had been developing it and knew it best. Warren had not explicitly given Cindy that authority, and with all his other technicians, he had done the actual writing of the proposal. He had assumed that once she was farther along, she would meet with him and discuss it, in order for him to write it. He had been making notes on the project, in order to write the draft when the time came. When Kikanza asked him about the project's schedule, he was shocked to learn that Cindy had almost completed her rough draft of the proposal.

3. What are each person's job responsibilities? To some extent, the question of authority overlaps with the question of responsibilities. In her previous job, Cindy and all other technicians had been responsible for writing the rough drafts of their work, which was then reviewed and refined by their supervisor. In Warren's unit, he had always done all the writing because he wrote more easily and more competently than the technicians. Cindy had felt that she would have been shirking her responsibility to neglect to write a rough draft. Warren had felt that Cindy had exceeded her authority by writing the rough draft.

How are job responsibilities determined? The responsibilities of each subordinate relate to the ways in which the subordinate is expected to contribute toward meeting the organization's goals. The overall goals of the organization are determined at the highest level of the organization; then these goals are analyzed into specific objectives for the organizational level immediately beneath.

Each subsequent level must then determine specific objectives for the next-lower level of the organization. Ultimately, it is the responsibility of the manager or supervisor to determine the work objectives for the subordinate, according to the objectives the manager has been given for the work unit by her or his superior.

The supervisor assumes that the subordinate will perform those functions by any means or procedures necessary or will request assistance in order to meet the responsibilities. These responsibilities are the work for which (a) the subordinate is held accountable and (b) the subordinate is given resources with which to perform the work. If the supervisor and the subordinate do not agree as to the breadth, depth, and performance criteria for these responsibilities, both the supervisor and the subordinate risk being seen as dodging responsibility. This leads to a decrease in the supervisor's confidence, and the working relationship may spiral downward as a result. This further hinders the performance of the supervisor's work unit.

4. What are the priorities for what should be done, and what actually gets done in this working relationship? This question actually relates mostly to *priorities* for action. In most jobs, many things need to be done. Of these numerous possibilities, a worker is unlikely to be able to do more than one at a time. Thus, some things must be done before other things. Clearly, the things that get done first should either be the first steps in a sequential task or the most important things. Superiors and subordinates almost always agree about which steps in a sequence should be done first. But they don't always agree about which procedures and projects are most important and should get done first.

While Cindy was working on the circuit-board project, a co-worker asked her to help him test a related project, which was in the final stages before going to quality control. Cindy was in the middle of figuring out a complicated procedure, so she asked her co-worker if he minded either waiting a while or asking someone else to help. What Cindy hadn't known was that Warren had specifically told the co-worker to ask for Cindy's help. Cindy was somewhat ahead of schedule on her project, and testing was always a top priority for Warren.

Fortunately for Cindy, her co-worker discreetly told her about Warren's feelings on testing and that he was pleased with Cindy's rapid progress on her project. Cindy stopped what she was doing and helped her co-worker, averting further obstacles to a good working relationship with Warren. Cindy also learned that for Warren, testing should be given more attention and other resources than other aspects of her job. Warren had communicated clearly to Cindy's co-worker Warren's priorities, so Cindy's co-worker was able to assert Warren's priorities confidently.

Priorities for time, attention, and other resources may need to be specified and negotiated in a working relationship, and changing circumstances may radically alter what those priorities should be. A clear focus on the organization's goals and the department's objectives help in that process.

5. How do things get done when new situations arise? Even in the most stable of business circumstances, new situations arise: People are hired and fired, get sick and get well, leave or retire. Equipment breaks and is repaired; supplies are used and restocked. Organizations acquire new clients and lose old ones. Suppliers go out of business, and new suppliers open up. Priorities change and are renegotiated. These are the times when the written rules and conventional procedures fail to work. These are the times when unwritten rules and hidden strategies come to the fore.

When the standard conventions don't work, new ways must be found to get the important work done. Supervisors and subordinates need to agree on guidelines for these exceptions. These guidelines must be sufficiently broad to allow latitude for multiple contingencies, but sufficiently specific to offer direction and avoid disorganized and counterproductive responses.

For example, when Warren found out about the impending potential freeze on equipment purchases, he had to figure out a way to adjust his budget to permit the purchase of the testing equipment sooner than he had planned to. He and Kikanza sat down and figured out how he could postpone some of his other purchases in order to have the money for it. Also, Kikanza met with a few of the other managers in her department and got them to postpone some of their purchases as well. They knew that Kikanza would do some reshifting back to them once Warren's department had rebounded from the equipment purchase.

Once Warren and Kikanza had come up with a general guideline for paring down current purchases, Warren had the guidance he needed to manage the day-to-day decisions about expenditures. The

Exercise.

To understand your own working relationships with your subordinates and your supervisors, explore your own answers to the five basic questions:

1. What do supervisors need from their subordinates in order to do their jobs?
   a. What do you need from your subordinates in order to do your job? Have you made clear what information you require from your subordinates? Do you make it easy for your subordinates to give you the information you need? (Are you accessible? Do you respond appropriately to their requests for help? Do you show a positive attitude toward learning from mistakes?) How else can you avoid being embarrassed that your subordinates don't keep you informed?
   b. What does your supervisor need from you in order to do her or his job? Do you make sure that your supervisor stays informed of the work you do and of what goes on in your work unit? Does your supervisor know when your work unit isn't able to do its job adequately? Does your supervisor know about mistakes you've made, as well as your successes?

2. What do subordinates need from their supervisors in order to do their jobs?
   a. What do your subordinates need from you in order to do their jobs? Because your subordinates are the experts in their jobs, they're in the best position to know what they need from you to improve their effectiveness. Do you make sure that you find out what they need and that, as much as possible, you supply it?
   b. What do you need from your supervisor in order to do your job? Are you giving your supervisor an opportunity to provide resources in order to avoid or avert problems in your work unit? Are there any resources your supervisor could provide that might improve your efficiency, effectiveness, or productivity?

3. What are each person's job responsibilities?
   a. What are your subordinates' job responsibilities? Do your subordinates know what you consider to be the breadth and depth of their responsibilities? Are they sure of the criteria you use to evaluate their performance?
   b. What are your job responsibilities? Would both your subordinates and your supervisor agree with your description of these?
   c. What are your supervisor's job responsibilities?

4. What are the priorities for what should be done, and what actually gets done in this working relationship?
   a. What do you think are the priorities for what should be done, and what do your subordinates actually do? Have you and your subordinates discussed this?
   b. What does your supervisor think are the priorities for what should be done, and what do you actually do? Do you and your supervisor agree about this?

5. How do things get done when new situations arise?
   a. What guidelines have you provided for your subordinates for handling new situations? Are they sufficiently broad to adapt to unexpected contingencies? Are they sufficiently specific to provide direction?
   b. What guidelines has your supervisor provided for you for handling new situations? Are they sufficiently broad, yet sufficiently specific?

How did you fare in relation to your supervisor and your subordinates? Are you and they largely in agreement? In what areas do you disagree? The next section of this chapter suggests a strategy for reaching greater agreement.

other managers in Kikanza's department did the same. Warren made sure that he showed the other work units his appreciation for their cooperation, so all work units benefited from the process.

Through our observation of these superior–subordinate working relationships, we identified the problem as being the result of ignorance, disagreement, and discord in this primary working relationship. We also found fractionation within work units and across departments.

The Solution

Once we had identified the problem, we needed to find a solution. After generating a number of possible alternatives and evaluating each, we settled on one solution: Arrange for a series of meetings during which supervisors and subordinates could work out their differences. Following these meetings, we determined that co-workers across and within work units could more readily work out their differences once supervisors and subordinates had reached greater accord. Thus, the co-workers within work units would meet later, in order to coordinate their actions and collaborate on strategies for helping the organization to respond effectively to constant change.

Next, we had to figure out a way to implement the solution. Again, we followed the three-step process of generating ideas, evaluating each idea, and choosing a single solution. Of course, we involved key personnel in the organization of these three processes. As a result of this three-step process, we decided on a strategy for helping subordinates and supervisors clarify their working relationships.

The implementation strategy:

1. Arrange for subordinates to meet, discuss, and understand the five key questions
2. Encourage subordinates to draft a statement of responsibilities
3. Guide subordinates to refine their statements
4. Arrange for individual meetings with a supervisor, an immediate subordinate, and an impartial third party, to negotiate agreement on the statements
5. Help each supervisor–subordinate pair to write a final version of the negotiated agreement
6. Arrange for meetings within each work unit, for team members to review the statements and negotiate agreement on any remaining issues

7. Have senior management review the final set of written statements, and compile them into a final published document

The Implementation

1. Discussing the Issues

We arranged to meet with small groups of subordinates to help them to discuss and understand the five key questions. These training sessions included all personnel from department-level managers through the CEO (over 100 managers in all). Our consultant-trainers used concrete examples for each of the questions as guides for helping the manager–subordinates understand the issues.

2. Writing the Drafts

We encouraged each manager–subordinate in the group to draft a written statement of responsibilities. Once the issues had been discussed, each subordinate considered personal answers to each of the questions. Then each subordinate drafted a statement of responsibility, detailing the answers to Question 3, alluding to some of the answers in Questions 1 and 2, and omitting the answers to Questions 4 and 5.

3. Refining the Statements

Once the subordinates had written their statements, we offered suggestions and refinements of their documents. They revised them, usually incorporating our suggestions, but occasionally deciding, after carefully considering them, not to follow them. After discussing these issues with the particular subordinates, we agreed with their decisions.

4. Negotiating the Issues

We arranged for a series of individual meetings between supervisors and their immediate subordinates, and we offered an impartial third party to be present during those meetings. At the meetings, the supervisor and the subordinate would each discuss their respective answers to the five basic questions. Then, with the help of the third party, they would negotiate an agreement about the answers to these questions.

Though Questions 4 (priorities) and 5 (novel situations) were not addressed in the written statements, the subordinates still discussed these issues with their supervisors. Agreement on these issues was settled verbally, as were some of the issues for Questions 1 and 2 (mutual needs). The answers to Question 3 (responsibilities), and some of those for Questions 1 and 2, were reconciled in the written statements.

As would be expected, the supervisors were more interested in negotiating answers to Question 1 (what supervisors need). They also generally wanted more cooperation and support from their subordinates than the subordinates believed necessary. The issues that the supervisors emphasized were their subordinates' need to keep abreast of changes in their areas of expertise and in technology related to their field, as well as changes relating to the organization as a whole—its goals, business practices, markets, and competition.

Because supervisors were generally responsible for budget planning (such as revenue projections, new business, and accuracy of cost estimates), they wanted immediate notification about any problems or operations that might affect budget planning. They also sought regularly scheduled planning sessions in which subordinates and their supervisor could share ideas and devise new strategies.

The subordinates, on the other hand, were more preoccupied with negotiating answers to Question 2 (what subordinates need), particularly regarding the authority they would be given. For example, they discussed access to secret and confidential information; appropriate limits for discretionary spending and appropriate latitude for their own budgets; authority to evaluate, reward, and discipline their subordinates, as well as authority to hire, fire, transfer, develop, train, and promote their subordinates; and latitude for negotiating with suppliers and clients.

Subordinates also cited some of the other resource issues described more fully in Chapter 6. Unsurprisingly, they reciprocated their supervisors' feelings of needing more support from their counterpart in the relationship.

On Question 3 (responsibilities), both supervisors and subordinates were concerned with functioning efficiently and effectively.

Both sought ways to "read from the same page of the same book" and to support each other. They discussed changing priorities and reasons for past problems and crises. This frank exchange of what each party expected of the other clarified some previously ambiguous issues and uncovered some areas of dispute. Although not all issues could be resolved at this session, they were brought to the surface and available for future discussions.

Questions 4 and 5 were raised and discussed to varying extent, depending on the urgency of the issues. In relationships that were overloaded with work, questions of priorities (Question 4) were discussed at length. In relationships that were having problems in dealing with unanticipated events (Question 5), questions about exceptional procedures were of special interest.

Our role throughout the negotiation was to ensure a balanced perspective and to confirm that all major issues were discussed in detail—particularly those related to Questions 4 and 5. The specific items of negotiation included the following:

1. Devise strategic and tactical plans

2. Review annual planning and budgeting cycles

3. Regular update and review of operations against budget with superior

4. Ensure, within approved plans and budgets, that direct reports have needed resources

5. Ensure that staffing and funding levels are reasonable in terms of recognized industry standards

6. Approve additions, transfer, termination, and replacement of staff

7. Communicate and coordinate up, down, and laterally

8. Provide staff with leadership, counseling, training, and opportunities to develop professionally

9. Approve expenditures within spending limits

10. Review and evaluate the performance of staff on a yearly basis

11. Maintain and administer, within guidelines, salary program

12. Keep superiors abreast of changes in technology and business practices in your area

13. Monitor competition and their products, services, and costs

14. Regularly assess and review quality of service

15. Manage assigned programs, products and services

The average bargaining session lasted about two hours, but the time devoted to each question varied, depending on the problems confronting the two parties. What specifically was written into the responsibility statement generally was discussed much less than the other issues, which would remain as unwritten inside information.

Responsibilities. For each statement of responsibility, supervisors and subordinates reached agreement on content, procedures, and timing. In many cases, responsibilities were changed from those proposed by the subordinate. For example, supervisors reassigned programs within their units from one subordinate to another. In addition, priorities were negotiated to focus attention on the critical needs of both parties. Both supervisors and subordinates talked about their needs for attention, support, and teamwork—especially their need for closer collaboration in turbulent times of changes.

Authority and Accountability. On each of the authority issues, the two parties negotiated limits and control procedures. Spending limits were evaluated in terms of risk and efficiency and in most cases were increased. Staffing authority was changed to reflect new responsibilities. Training, performance review, and salary administration were specified as management decision areas, supported by staff functions. Finally, procedures for assuring accountability of the subordinate to the supervisor were specified.

Working Relationship. The final area of negotiation was their working relationship. Subordinates generally sought closer collaboration with supervisors, including greater information, influence, and support. They wanted to grow professionally and be promoted. Supervisors typically were more concerned with accountability and being kept informed, but they made it clear that if their subordinates worked to promote their supervisors, in return, the supervisors would help the subordinates to outgrow their jobs.

The final step for the supervisors and subordinates was to negotiate a mutually acceptable *written* statement of responsibility about their working relationship.

5. Signing the Agreement

Once the two parties had agreed in substance, we helped each subordinate to make the appropriate revisions to the statement of the negotiated mutual agreement. Then we served as impartial witnesses to the signing and dating of the contract by both parties. On the occasion of the signing, the contract became effectively part of the written documentation of the organization, and it was executed by sending copies of it to the proper administrative offices.

Though the written statement related mostly to Question 3, in order to come to consensus about it, Questions 1, 2, 4, and 5 needed to have been discussed and negotiated as well. Some of the answers to Questions 1 and 2 were actually included in the written statement, but none of the answers to Questions 4 and 5 were included.

6. Building the Teams

Once all of the written statements of agreement between individual subordinates and supervisors had been signed and dated, we needed to resolve issues remaining among co-workers within work units and across departments. We arranged for additional meetings within each work unit, in which all team members reviewed the statements and negotiated to resolve any remaining disagreements between team members. The work unit negotiations ensured that all members of the team had the opportunity to clarify issues, consider potential problems, and discuss co-worker collaborative relationships.

7. Finalizing the Document

Senior management reviewed the final set of written statements, and they were compiled into a published document. Once all of the statements were agreed to by all members of a work unit and all co-workers at each management level, senior management reviewed the final version of the entire document. That document was then published and made available to all participants.

Beyond the Written Document

Revelation of Inside Information

By the end of this process, the newly updated standardized methods and routine conventions were written and formalized. But far more happened during this process than the updating of the written rules and conventional procedures. In addition to the written document that updated what people were expected to do on their jobs, this process also revealed many hidden strategies and unwritten rules. In the negotiation sessions, much more information was exchanged than appeared in the signed document. In fact, interpretation of these signed responsibility statements depends on this inside information.

These two- or three-page documents were designed only to serve as buoys in the sea of understandings between the two parties. Whenever some dispute about these matters arises, the two parties can refer to this document to sharpen their discussion. One senior manager was grateful that "this procedure took these issues out of hearsay and gave us something more substantial to work with."

Concealment of Inside Information

Why did the newly updated unwritten rules and hidden strategies remain undocumented? One reason they weren't recorded was that their very nature is fluid and constantly changing in response to changes in personnel, the marketplace, resources, and other factors.

Nonetheless, even if it were practical to record these, they wouldn't have been recorded. Most inside information has to do with *people*: Who is effective in doing what? What increases their effectiveness? Who isn't as effective? How is their productivity maximized while their ineffectiveness is minimized? Clearly, these kinds of secrets of the organization should be shared discreetly and only with those who know how to profit from using the information to everyone's advantage, not to hurt or upset anyone. (Recall the repercussions that occurred in Broderick MacNeil's firm in Chapter 3—the disclosure of personnel evaluations upset morale and disrupted the effective functioning of the organization.)

Other kinds of secrets also might be ill used if they were recorded in print. If competing organizations, clients, or suppliers became aware of these, the organization might be harmed as a result. For example, if you heard of a clever covert strategy used by a competitor to gain a competitive edge, you'd be foolish not to try it yourself, to eliminate that competitive advantage. Your competitor would be equally unwise to record these strategies in writing and thereby risk your discovery of them.

Other hidden strategies involve differential treatment of some suppliers and some clients. This may happen either because the situational context dictates unusual treatment or because such treatment builds ties in the collegial competence network. However, as a client, if you became aware that another client had received a discount, added services or benefits, extended credit options, or some other special treatment, you would not be pleased, regardless of the context in which the other client was given these advantages. As a supplier, if you found out that another supplier received either more money for the same product or service or the same money for a less valuable product or service, your relationship with the organization would be injured.

The Outcomes of the Process

Significant changes were brought about by this process. This organization developed a management structure that was a better fit than the previous one, which had been more appropriate to an organization half its size. In the process, new teams were formed, additional responsibilities were created, and greater authority was delegated further down the hierarchy. What had been ambiguous became clarified. What had been impossibly out of date became current.

During the process, important features of the organization emerged that had previously been hidden from view: They addressed how things were really done and how subordinates, supervisors, and peers really worked together. Subordinates needed to convey to their supervisors and to some of their peers that their jobs were both more complicated and more difficult than the written documents and conventional procedures indicated. They needed their supervisors to see these hidden features of their jobs so that they would receive support. Supervisors used this opportunity to tell subordinates about the complexity of their jobs and their needs for information and support that went far beyond the written descriptions. Moreover, the hidden negative consequences of a supervisor's being surprised were often dramatically illustrated for subordinates. Each side revealed hidden aspects of their work that helped the other side to understand the reasons for apparently unreasonable actions in the past. Finally, this process served to focus both parties' attention on collaboration to produce results.

Summary

This case study revealed (1) how outdated the written rules and conventional procedures can become if they don't include strategies for updating them, and (2) how a program for updating them can help. This particular program, which focused on the working relationships among unit members, asked five important questions: (1) What do supervisors need from subordinates in order to do their jobs? (2) What do subordinates need from their supervisors in order to do their jobs? (3) What are the subordinate's responsibilities? (4) What are the priorities for what should be done, and what actually gets done? (5) How do things get done when new situations arise?

Though the answers to all five questions generally are not included in the organization's written documentation, all of these questions must be discussed and resolved if working relationships are to be effective. Thus, the written and the unwritten rules, and the conventional and extraordinary strategies complement one another. Seek information about and insight into both in order to improve your effectiveness and to enhance your career.

Many people claim to be too busy with day-to-day problems to take time to uncover the hidden features of their job situations, much less negotiate guidelines to action with competent colleagues on the job. As one harried executive told me, "We're too busy fighting fires around here to put our feet up and talk about fire prevention." I suggested that unless they discovered the hidden conditions that ignited their fires, they should buy better firefighting equipment.

The next chapter describes more specifically how you can become a more effective leader. Chapter 9 focuses on the working relationship between supervisors and subordinates, viewed from the perspective of the supervisor.

9

Develop Fast-Track Leadership

For Managers and Managers-to-Be

This chapter has been written from the perspective of managers, describing how they can help their subordinates to move onto the fast track. However, if you are not yet a manager, you will still benefit from reading this. Understanding the manager's perspective may help you to become one much more quickly. Also, by learning some of the reasons for managers to encourage their subordinates to move to the fast track, you may get some ideas for inspiring your supervisor to encourage you. Put on your boss's shoes and take a short walk with him.

Trouble on the Fast Track

Katrina Mendeleyev, a young manager of a Fortune 500 company, who had completed her MBA a few years earlier, complained that she felt she had failed as a manager. Although she was on the fast track in her organization, Katrina wanted to transfer back into her old job as an internal consultant. She knew that this move would hurt her career progress, but she had tried everything she could think of to solve her managerial problem, and nothing seemed to work.

Katrina was responsible for staffing a departmental data center that operated around the clock, seven days a week. This meant that she supervised four different shifts of workers, among whom there seemed to be little or no communication. Problems that surfaced on one shift were not reported to the next shift. Hence, small and routine problems escalated into major crises. The effectiveness of the data center as a whole was adversely affected as mounting problems were left unresolved from one shift to the next.

Katrina appealed to her subordinates by every means, from gentle to tough, but nothing she did made any difference. Not one of her subordinates saw it as a personal job responsibility to respond to problems or to communicate them from one shift to the next. Even many of the early warning signs of developing problems were not clearly specified as anyone's responsibility. Thus, subordinates could legitimately avoid taking corrective action by claiming that it was not part of their written job descriptions. They could safely avoid the added hours and additional aggravation of getting involved in solving a problem by simply ignoring it.

Katrina was learning the harsh lesson that not all workers want to outgrow their narrowly prescribed job descriptions. Some people prefer to do only the minimum required. They see their job as secure and their job rewards as fixed. The hope of future career payoffs for expanding responsibilities and capabilities is not for them. Attempts by a manager to make this possibility salient to them usually are rejected.

Find the Few

If you cannot motivate everyone, can you motivate a few? Yes. Katrina needed at least one enthusiastic subordinate on each of the four shifts. Once she could identify at least one person on each shift, she could work with those four subordinates by investing her resources in their careers, as described in Chapter 3.

Much to Katrina's surprise, concentrating her resources on a few who were eager to outgrow their present jobs paid tremendous dividends. Within six months, her four shift leaders had outgrown their former jobs to such a degree that her formerly intensive level of supervision became superfluous. Based on this improved effectiveness, Katrina proposed a restructuring in which the shift leaders were upgraded to a supervisory position. Because her data center's productivity had increased, Katrina's supervisor thought such a recommendation was advisable, and the four shift leaders—and Katrina—were promoted.

Katrina had successfully used a hidden strategy for leadership, which I call "Fast-Track Leadership." *Fast-track leadership* ("FTL") creates and delivers career opportunities to those who earnestly seek career growth. However, although this process augments the documented, conventional career development programs, it usually remains hidden in the context of day-to-day activities. Many people spend their entire careers within organizations and never experience the hidden power of this strategy for leadership—whether as a supervisor or as a subordinate. This chapter describes some of the important components of FTL.

Four Features of Fast-Track Leadership (FTL)

FTL expands the total capability of an organizational unit because the leaders invest in the careers of the subordinates who yearn to outgrow their present jobs. This reciprocal process of leaders' investment and subordinates' growth works much as apprenticeships do. The process allows both subordinates and supervisors to successfully accomplish complicated and difficult tasks despite apparent obstacles and impedances.

The leader and the selected apprentices do this by collaborating to capitalize on both the hidden opportunities and resources of the work units and the unique mix of abilities and motivations of people within and around the work unit. Thus, separate individual workers become integrated into cohesive, coordinated, and adaptable teams at the level of the work unit and into larger collaborative competence networks at the level of the organization.

Thus, four key features of FTL stand out:

1. *Growth.* Some subordinates want to outgrow their present jobs and written job descriptions.

2. *Investment.* Supervisors who want to encourage these subordinates do so by investing resources in the careers of those subordinates.

3. *Focus.* Because supervisors have limited resources, they target those resources more specifically toward those subordinates who clearly communicate their interest in outgrowing their present job descriptions.

4. *Integration.* To be maximally effective, supervisors and the targeted subordinates integrate to form cohesive teams within the work unit and collaborative networks of competent co-workers throughout the organization.

How FTL Works

As the head of the division's new data center, Katrina continues to apply the FTL strategies for leadership. She also now shows her shift managers to do likewise. Katrina, moreover, practices FTL strategies with her supervisors, her peers, and her co-workers, and she instructs her shift managers in how to use FTL, as well.

Growth. Katrina and the managers she leads continually seek to expand the total capability of their organizational unit by encouraging their individual subordinates to outgrow their written job descriptions.

Investment. Katrina and her managers encourage this by investing in the careers of those individual subordinates who demonstrate their willingness to outgrow their jobs. They begin the investment process by tapping into the subordinates' individual motivations to broaden their interests from their present job duties and responsibilities into the wider interests of their future careers and of the larger organization. Thus, if a leader wants to entice a subordinate to outgrow the present job description, the leader must create and offer career advancement opportunities that are distinctly superior to those of the existing job.

Focus. Initially, the shift managers encouraged all of their subordinates to outgrow their present jobs. Katrina noticed this pattern and warned her managers not to make the same mistake she did: She advised the shift leaders to target their career investments toward specific people on each shift. Deciding whom to target should be based on the unique set of abilities and motivations of the available people, thereby capitalizing on the hidden opportunities and resources of the unit. This selective investment process may require some strategic planning, in which the expertise and resources of each person are evaluated against the context of the work unit.

Also, even after a leader had begun to invest in a few subordinates, several factors could prompt a leader to discontinue that investment. For example, one of the swing shift employees started having trouble meeting even the minimal requirements of the existing job; thus, he stopped being a candidate for investment. Further, a couple of subordinates seemed to express less enthusiasm for doing so once they realized that they might not be "one of the guys" as much as they had been before. A few more of the subordinates failed to demonstrate their ability to outgrow their present jobs, so the leaders no longer urged them to do so.

Nonetheless, Katrina advised the managers to always be ready to change their minds if the subordinate changed. Given a satisfactory level of performance on the existing job, any time that a competent subordinate expresses an interest in outgrowing the present job, the leader should be open to advising the subordinate on how to do so.

Integration. The way in which the leaders invested in their subordinates enlarged the subordinates' jobs in ways that integrated the individual members of the work unit into cohesive, coordinated, and adaptable teams. Ultimately, the work unit teams likewise became integrated into larger collaborative competence networks. Competence networks are described more fully in Chapter 6.

Anyone may use FTL: (a) Your supervisor may use it to enlarge the capability of your department, (b) you may use it to improve your influence in related departments, and (c) your subordinates may use it to improve their effectiveness and promotability within your work unit.

Change Offers an Opportunity for Leadership

The Chance for Change

Chico Cervantes had been in his position as the director of an information systems division of a large multinational clothing company for two and a half years. He felt that he had mastered the job and was eager to outgrow it to become one of the organization's vice presidents. When he became aware of top management's intent to install a new computer-controlled cutting machine, he realized that it would greatly improve the efficiency of the organization's operations. Seeing this as a tremendous opportunity for him to advance in his career, Chico requested to be put in charge of the project.

Much to his surprise, however, he was refused the new position because his superiors felt his present position already required the majority of his time. Not willing to accept defeat, Chico put in a second request for the position, informing his superiors that he was fully capable of taking on the additional responsibilities. After much negotiation, management finally agreed to give Chico a chance and assigned him as head of the new project.

The Status Quo: Chaos and Crisis

Before this project came up, Chico had been very much at the center of his work unit. He would receive direct questions and requests from all 20 of his professionals and all 12 of his staff people, in addition to numerous executives and outside colleagues, clients, and suppliers. He maintained an open door, and everyone was welcomed by Chico. All matters came to him for resolution, and he enjoyed being at the center of all of this activity. On the surface, he was very much in control of his division.

However, in terms of the unwritten rules and hidden strategies of his division, Chico was not in control. With only one chief and many workers, it was exceedingly difficult to schedule projects and to maintain high technical standards. For example, Ruth Goldstein, a whiz on scheduling, was constantly struggling to meet most of Chico's promised completion date and budget estimates. She was often forced to beg project supervisors to help her out of tight spots. Similarly, Tambuzi Nkrumah, a technical genius, grew increasingly impatient that technical standards were not applied uniformly and documentation was erratic. Many workers felt that they were constantly in crisis, living with chaos.

To cope with the crises and the chaos, Chico's subordinates had developed their own procedures for getting things done. These hidden strategies allowed them to function—often in spite of Chico's unrealistic estimates for schedules and costs. Some of his promised completion dates and cost estimates could be renegotiated with clients, but others could not. Some of his agreements with people within the division could be modified if the persons concerned were agreeable, but others could not.

With increasing frequency, key people cooperated to get projects done—even at the cost of their own work. Periodically, even managers and supervisors would pitch in and write program language or work on the systems. They would lend people to the project most in trouble and hope that the favor would be returned. With all of this effort, they were still barely keeping up with most of Chico's promises to users.

Many had repeatedly asked Chico to stop making promises without first consulting Ruth about scheduling and Tambuzi about technical standards. But Chico did not listen. He thought that the way to move up in his organization was to do more and to increase the number of his responsibilities. Thus, he told his subordinates to hire more people to get the work done. They did this, but they couldn't use the new people effectively because they lacked the time to train them or to do all other things that are necessary to make them effective contributors.

Chico had risen through the ranks due to his technical expertise, but he had failed to appreciate the value of learning the unwritten rules and the hidden strategies in the process. He did not understand that his control practices were working at odds with this inside information and that his subordinates were burning out as a result.

The Impetus for Change

Chico knew that in order to perform effectively in both of his positions, it would be crucial that he make more efficient use of his time. He figured that he needed to save 50 percent of his present work time to run the department once the new equipment was in operation. Even more time than this would be required during the early start-up stages. Thus, Chico needed to cut his present job activities by 50 percent. Chico called my consulting partners and me for help.

After examining Chico's division and talking to key people, we concluded that if he was to save 50 percent of his time from his present duties, he needed to develop FTL. By using FTL, he could develop the leadership of some of his subordinates to help pick up the other 50 percent of his duties. To use FTL effectively, Chico had to outgrow his present job, using the three-phased process for outgrowing a job. (Chapter 5 more fully describes this process, from the perspective of a subordinate.)

Role-Finding

To begin with, Chico needed to identify a group of key people who would be interested in taking on added responsibilities of the work unit, thus relieving Chico of some of his duties. Once these key people were identified, we asked them to provide information about their job and about their supervisor, using the five questions described in Chapter 8: (1) What does Chico need from you in order to do his job effectively? (2) What do you need from Chico in order to do your job well? (3) What are your job responsibilities? (4) What are the priorities for what should be done, and what actually gets done on your job? and (5) How do things really get done on your job when new situations arise?

After answering the questions, the key people spoke with us and with Chico about the results. The information was then used to negotiate how responsibilities would be distributed in their department, using the same process described in Chapter 8.

Role-Making

The negotiation process began with Chico and two of his key people, Ruth and Tambuzi. Ruth was a capable project manager who could handle effectively the details of many projects at the same time and get projects completed on time and on budget. Tambuzi, in contrast, was able to solve complex technical problems and to establish technical standards to implement his solutions. Although neither Ruth nor Tambuzi was very good at the other's specialty, they complemented each other very well.

Chico, Ruth, and Tambuzi agreed that Ruth would assume primary responsibility for all of the scheduling in the division and Tambuzi would take on all of the technical issues. Chico would retain overall responsibility for the management of the division, including relationships with higher-level management and with other departments. Chico's strong suit was his ability to convince executives and peers in other departments that new and improved computer services would be cost-beneficial to them. He had a strong record of successfully upgrading the computer use of both the executives and the departments parallel to his own.

During the negotiation, Chico, Ruth, and Tambuzi agreed that Chico would cease dealing with upper management and with other departments on scheduling and technical matters. Instead, he would sell the general concept for improved computer service and then turn the proposed project over to Ruth and Tambuzi to work out the scheduling and technical details.

This change in how things were to be done required all three parties to learn new strategies. Ruth and Tambuzi had to develop expertise not only on scheduling and technical matters, respectively, but also on how to negotiate with people in other departments and in the executive suite. Chico had to learn how to defer to Ruth on scheduling and to Tambuzi on technical matters. In fact, during these negotiations, Chico realized that his previous practice of negotiating all of the details of new projects with other departments had actually been less effective because he didn't have the firm grasp on scheduling and technical matters that Ruth and Tambuzi had.

Fortunately for Ruth and Tambuzi, Chico's career opportunity supplied a strong incentive for him not only to see a better way to operate but also to try to implement it. Chico agreed to allow and support the growth of Ruth into an effective scheduling manager and the growth of Tambuzi into an effective technical manager. He agreed to invest in their careers by (a) guiding their training, (b) deferring to them at the appropriate moments when developing new business, and (c) referring questions and requests to them that came from people inside or outside of the division, instead of handling them all himself as he had in the past.

By allowing Ruth and Tambuzi to handle the new responsibilities, Chico provided them with the authority to deal with these matters. Thus, it was extremely important that Chico did not take any actions that would undermine Ruth's and Tambuzi's authority, such as revising a decision that Ruth or Tambuzi had already made.

In addition to these added responsibilities, Chico also agreed to change the reporting relationships in the department, so that Ruth and Tambuzi would each be in charge of five project supervisors who had previously reported to Chico. As part of their responsibilities, Ruth and Tambuzi would evaluate the performance of these supervisors and make salary recommendations for them, which Chico would review. Thus, by delegating these responsibilities to Ruth and Tambuzi, Chico would save some of the time he needed in order to take on the new project.

After the new responsibilities were negotiated among Chico and Ruth and Tambuzi, they agreed that Ruth and Tambuzi would each hold negotiation sessions with each of the project supervisors whom they supervised. These negotiation sessions were similar to those they had undergone with Chico. Thus, Ruth and Tambuzi negotiated how responsibilities would be assigned to each member of their work teams. Chico reviewed and approved the results of these negotiations.

The negotiation sessions offered an opportunity for all members of the unit to propose new ways of doing things to increase their effectiveness and to enhance their career opportunities. Team members suggested many new ways of improving communications, coordination, and teamwork. They placed new emphasis on career development opportunities by making this a high priority and by legitimizing their chances to outgrow their jobs. These suggestions were discussed, and appropriate statements were written into the responsibility statements.

The results of this process were gratifying to Chico. Although he had to give up the feeling that he controlled everything that happened in his division, he gained a more flexible and effective division. Simultaneously, he realized the net 50 percent savings of his time that he needed in order to take on the new project.

Role-Implementing

As a result of the negotiated changes, Chico was able to see how FTL could allow his subordinates to effectively use his organization's unwritten rules and hidden strategies. When he allowed his subordinates to do so, they capitalized on the opportunity and turned his department into a far more effective collaborative team of productive workers.

Chico's subordinates had grown weary of his old style of leadership. They eagerly welcomed the opportunity to negotiate some strategies that would reduce their stress on the job. Though they knew that periodic crises were part of their work, they also understood how to remain somewhat flexible to deal with these crises. Under the new system, people were encouraged to outgrow their jobs and to get their work done, and they acknowledged the desirability of teamwork in handling multiple projects.

The plan that was developed through this process capitalized on the unique abilities and motivations of the members of the division. Chico flourished in applying his strength—his development of new business for the division—having delegated to Ruth and Tambuzi his weakness—scheduling and technical matters. Both Ruth and Tambuzi similarly expanded on their strengths and delegated to their subordinates those tasks for which they lacked expertise. Project supervisors, in their turns, also developed what they did best, and they delegated other tasks to *their* subordinates.

Continued Coordinated Responsivity to Change

The negotiated plan for Chico's division called for flexibility to allow the division to deal with constantly changing demands. Ruth was given procedures to help keep people coordinated or at least informed as priorities were changed in response to new demands from inside or outside of the department. Tambuzi was given the latitude to change technical guidelines when specified exceptions occurred.

In addition to this plan, all parties involved acknowledged that they must function as a team; they'd succeed or fail together. They understood that blaming one another for failures would not help them succeed. This spirit of cooperation had an added benefit: Once Chico was promoted to vice president, Tambuzi and Ruth continued to share their complementary roles as the technical and administrative managers of the division. Chico Cervantes was a creative guy looking for a method—and he found it.

Chico's case is an example of how a manager can use FTL to transform a one-chief department into a team-oriented one. The series of negotiations had helped to clarify the written rules and guidelines for following standard procedures. These helped everyone in the division to deal with stable, routine, and repetitive activities. Further, they had uncovered numerous hidden strategies and unwritten rules, which helped them to respond quickly and successfully to changes within the organization and outside of it. And they reaped generous benefits for having done so.

Thus, the entire division increased the contributions of available talents and motivations of people. They developed and solidified standard procedures for handling standard situations, and they produced guidelines and strategies for handling the changes going on around them. In this way, they maintained both adequate flexibility and adequate control during periods of change.

What You Need in Order to Use FTL

In implementing role-making with a subordinate, it is important that you have (a) adequate latitude in task assignment and a reason to exercise it, (b) reasonably attractive resources, and the knowledge to apply them, (c) at least one subordinate who has job growth potential (ability) and the motivation to accept challenges beyond the present job, and (d) your own motivation and expertise for engaging in this process. When these conditions are met, you can use role-making to transform your unit into a more effective collaborative team, thereby helping your subordinates and you to successfully outgrow your present jobs.

Latitude in Job Assignments. At one extreme, you may not be able to give special assignments to your subordinates. Without adequate latitude in task assignment, you and your subordinates are deprived of the motivational and learning potential of providing satisfying work experiences—the intrinsic value of learning and performing challenging and interesting tasks. You might be unable to offer special assignments for several reasons: (a) the organization enforces its rigid written role definitions and forbids deviations from conventions in tasks assignment; (b) people in the work unit maintain fixed definitions of their jobs and reject opportunities for professional growth; (c) peers and superiors believe in having fixed jobs, equating changes in role definitions with ineffective management and the loss of control; or (d) tasks cannot be divided in ways that are compatible with the work unit's talents and motivations.

Adequate Career-Enhancing Resources. To successfully implement your role as supervisor, you also need to have adequate resources with which to support special assignments and to reward role-making behavior. These resources must be (a) attractive to the team member and (b) available at your exclusive discretion to determine when and in whom those resources are invested.

Two factors are involved in the resources question: motivation and support. You need adequate resources in order to motivate your subordinates to try to outgrow their jobs. Once you have inspired them to do so, you need adequate resources in order to support them in their efforts to do so. If you lack attractive positional resources, you can't (a) transform difficult assignments into challenging yet doable professional growth experiences, and (b) convert an added task assignment into a personally and professionally rewarding experience.

Without adequate resources to support achievement of complex and demanding tasks, your subordinates may either fail in their efforts or wane in their enthusiasm for persevering. Chapter 6 describes more fully the ways in which resources can encourage subordinates to outgrow their present jobs.

Motivated and Capable Subordinate. To implement FTL with your subordinates, at least one of your subordinates must possess (a) the potential ability to grow and (b) the motivation to accept job challenges beyond the present positions. Rarely is this the true cause for FTL not to work. In almost any work situation, at least one subordinate both has the ability to grow and would have the motivation to outgrow the present job description, given interesting *challenges*, adequate *encouragement* from their leader, and adequate *resources* for tackling them.

Support and Encouragement from Superiors. In order to use FTL effectively, you must have encouragement and support from your own superior. The resource and investment costs of implementing FTL vary according to the compatibility between this activity and the organization's management philosophy. People in organizations with extremely authoritarian philosophies of management experience investment costs much higher than those in organizations with more participative philosophies. Thus, unfortunately, fast-track leadership is found less often in authoritarian companies.

Motivated and Able Leader. Perhaps most important for this process, you must have both the motivation and the ability to implement FTL with your subordinates. Even if you have the four aforementioned elements, without motivation and ability, you cannot implement FTL with your subordinates: For latitude in task assignment to be useful, you must see a reason to exercise that latitude in assigning tasks. To make effective use of available resources, you must want to invest the resources you have. To develop a subordinate's potential for growth, you must believe in that person's potential and have the inclination to develop it.

You may, however, feel that you have the motivation, but you lack the expertise. This book can help you to develop your expertise in using FTL. If you also lack sufficient motivation, the next section may persuade you to gain it.

Why You Need to Use FTL

Why should you use FTL with your subordinates? It's hoped that this book has already shown you that FTL will clearly help you to outgrow your present leadership role and to develop leadership in your subordinates in order to outgrow it. But what if you like your present job and your present job situation? What if you don't want to outgrow your own present leadership? What are other reasons to develop FTL? Five reasons immediately surface:

1. Stress management and reduction for yourself and for your subordinates

2. Improved morale for your subordinates—and thereby for yourself

3. Response to extraordinary tasks

4. Response to changing circumstances

5. Outdistancing your competition

1. Stress management and reduction for yourself and for your subordinates. Most supervisors quickly realize that they can't do everything. If they try to do everything, they fail, their work unit fails, and they suffer from tremendous stress and anxiety in the process. They "burn out" and lose interest in their work, ceasing to enjoy any aspect of it. Supervisors need their subordinates to help them do their jobs well. Therefore, most effective supervisors enlist the aid of at least some of their subordinates.

2. Improved morale for your subordinates—and thereby for yourself. Most employees need to feel that they have opportunities for growth and advancement in order to enjoy tackling the tasks of their present jobs. Once they feel that they have reached dead ends, their productivity plummets. In addition to the negative effects of low productivity in the work unit, the supervisor's own morale also declines when the subordinates feel dissatisfied in their work. They may begin to feel more like prison guards than like managers.

3. Response to extraordinary tasks. Some work units have highly routine simple, repetitive tasks most of the time. Others have a widely diverse range of tasks, requiring everything from simple processing to the unique development of highly complex and intricate procedures for each project. Though the degree of variation in task complexity and diversity differs widely from one work unit to another, each work unit almost inevitably faces extraordinary and challenging assignments that require more than the routine procedures.

All supervisors and managers engage in some FTL when faced with overwhelming task demands. They collaborate with subordinates and exchange resources with them in order to complete special assignments. Competent supervisors prepare the work unit to be ready to accomplish these extraordinary tasks, so they invest in their subordinates ahead of time—before the crisis strikes.

4. Response to changing circumstances. Just as some industries and some departments have more complex and diverse tasks than others, they also have different amounts of change to which they must adapt. But no organization exists anywhere that does not experience some change, either within the organization or due to changes outside it. The resources (including personnel) available to the organization or to the department change; the products or services expected from it change; the guidelines for work processes and procedures change.

To adapt to these changing needs or changing resources, new strategies must be developed if the work unit is to succeed. These adaptations require extraordinary performance from the subordinates, who are unlikely to exceed their conventional job descriptions unless they receive extraordinary investment from their supervisors.

5. Outdistancing your competition. By developing and using FTL strategies, you gain the competitive edge. You can move ahead of other managers, even those who may have greater expertise in their present job than you do. Develop and use FTL to surpass even the most brilliant of conventional managers.

Adapting to Change

Adapting to change requires the invention of new ways of doing things. However, for an organization to function effectively, it must operate through coordinated actions of collaborative teams. Therefore, the organization needs to have some standard guidelines and routine procedures in order to smooth the way for integrating the efforts of all the individuals within the organization.

How can an organization balance its need for integrated, united action and its need for inventing new strategies in order either to improve or to adapt to change? People in the organization can't be allowed to spontaneously create new ways of doing everything whenever they feel like it; the lack of cohesion and the misguided originality could destroy the organization. Management would be impossible. Even if it could somehow be coordinated, many of the innovations wouldn't work, would duplicate the efforts of others, would waste valuable resources, or would be counterproductive.

On the other hand, if no one is allowed to invent new ways of doing things, the organization becomes rigidly unable to adapt; it mutates into a nonfunctional bureaucracy, or it withers and dies. Recent examples spring to mind: huge industries gone bankrupt, hundreds of plants shut down, entire communities wiped out because the local employer closed its doors.

Alternative Solutions: Rigidity or Ambiguity

Each organization must choose its own solution to this dilemma, but the best solutions lie somewhere between the extremes of chaos (everyone inventing new ways) and bureaucracy (no one inventing new ways). Many organizations resolve this by specifying that only executives should be allowed to invent new ways of getting things done. Unfortunately, executives don't always have the time or the expertise or the necessary information and other resources to do so. If less-than-competent people create new ways of getting things done, the results can be disastrous.

To handle this predicament, many organizations leave the answer ambiguously undefined. For example, an organization may officially let only a few people invent new ways of doing things while seldom enforcing the rule. The result of this ambiguity is that those who are more concerned with covering their tails do not invent and those who are more concerned with effectiveness do. In either case, the risks for error are great. If the invention pays off, the organization can say that they were wise not to discourage it. If it fails, the organization can blame the inventor and point to the rule prohibiting invention.

As a manager in an ambiguous context, you must sometimes decide whether to put your career in jeopardy to get things done, risking the wrath of your superiors if you make a mistake. It may seem more prudent to follow the old (irrelevant) rules and fail rather than invent new ways and succeed. However, if your organization rewards the bureaucratic manager for playing it safe and punishes the competent manager for taking a risk, its ability to adapt is limited. Given the turbulence of our times, you may need to seriously consider whether you want to choose obedient loyalty to an inflexible organization. Playing it safe might lead to an insecure future.

As organizations grow in size and complexity, the trade-off between chaos and bureaucracy becomes increasingly important. There is no simple answer. The competent must be allowed to experiment and make mistakes, and the less competent should be encouraged to follow the established procedures. When the competent find a better way to do something, it should be written down for others to follow.

Alternatives: Exceptions or New Standards

Two alternative ways of handling this perplexity are shown by the story of a team of three Australians and two Japanese engineers who installed a new Japanese-designed generator in an Australian plant. The installation was supposed to take two weeks, but the organization wanted it on line in one. One of the Australian engineers invented a way to install the machine in one week. All five engineers agreed that it would work.

Nonetheless, the Japanese engineers insisted on following the standard procedure. After the installation, the Japanese engineer wrote up the new procedure and sent it back to the home plant for use in future installations. It became the new established procedure. The Australian engineers, however, simply forgot about the proposed new invention and went on to a new project.

The two companies clearly had different resolutions for the comparative trade-offs of invention versus conformity: The Australian company allowed innovation on an ad hoc basis but did not encourage changes in standard procedures. The Japanese company did not permit ad hoc innovation but encouraged changes in standard procedures when the changes were effective.

Similarly, you must decide when and with whom in your work unit you will encourage inventions for handling unusual situations or extraordinary tasks. And you must determine for yourself when you will invent new strategies or write unauthorized rules instead of following the conventional procedures or written policies. For example, if you don't have the resources you need to fully develop FTL within your work unit, you may decide to invent modifications for implementing it.

The opportunities for invention are infinite, but the appropriate circumstances in which you'll decide to use it are much more limited. Apply your knack for invention to think of ways to use FTL for building a strong collaborative team within your work unit.

Applying FTL to Job Functions: Negotiable Issues

A new way to look at your present job situation is to assume that your organizational unit contains unrecognized responsibilities, authority, and resources. The activities listed in Table 9.1 illustrate some of the many tasks and functions of a work unit, though certainly not all of the possible tasks and functions. In order to effectively use the responsibilities, authority, and resources within your work unit, you must follow a three-step strategy:

1. Read the written rules, and find out about the conventional procedures for fulfilling responsibilities and for using authority and resources.

2. Investigate the existing unwritten rules and hidden strategies about each of these.

3. Negotiate with the members of your work unit, to maximize the effective use of each of these.

Responsibilities

Seek to identify in detail the responsibilities of each member of your work unit. Begin by looking for written descriptions of those responsibilities in the organization's documentation. However, because most work units are functionally connected with a number of other units and operate in a changing environment, the written list of responsibilities will be subject to different interpretations. Further, many of your subordinates may already have intuitively started using insider strategies for negotiating changes in their job responsibilities. (Recall how differently your own job description looked after doing the activities in Chapters 1 and 5.)

Table 9.1 The Tasks of a Work Unit

Conventional Function	Hidden Function
• Accept official responsibilities of unit	• Negotiate functional responsibilities with appropriate others
• Establish official authority over resources of unit	• Negotiate instrumental value of resources with appropriate others
• Assign tasks to positions according to official practices	• Tailor task assignments to particular people
• Train people to follow official practices	• Implement on-the-job training (a) challenging task assignments (b) resource investments (c) discussions
• Reward and punish people according to official due process	• Enact merit compensation (a) contributions (b) inducements
• Establish objectives within official strategic plan and implement programs to achieve objectives	• Enact strategic management process with others
• Monitor program progress and intervene as necessary to stay on time and on budget	• Enact program progress feedback with others
• Coordinate boundary-spanning activities of unit	• Negotiate with others networking activities
• Manage effectiveness, employing goals and objectives	• Negotiate with multiple constituencies

Once you've ascertained the conventional job responsibilities of your subordinates, you should look for their hidden responsibilities. Uncover these by focusing on your particular intermix of people, examining what they do, and where, when, with whom, and how they do it. This will expand and broaden the true set of responsibilities for each subordinate; these more realistic responsibilities are less open to misinterpretation by you or your subordinate.

Next, you are ready to negotiate the responsibilities of your work unit, not in terms of universals, but in terms of a particular time and situation. You and they acknowledge your interdependence and agree upon a working definition of your respective responsibilities. Encourage them to negotiate (not just accept) their responsibilities with you and with their co-workers in each unit. This is not a one-time fix; it continues as responsibilities and priorities change.

Authority and Resources

Another task is to determine who has authority to use your unit's resources. The written policies and procedures provide you with a good starting place for finding these. Each of your subordinates is authorized to use specified resources (people in positions, material in inventory, and capital in budgets) within certain constraints.

Do not, however, accept the official statement as definitive; explore more realistically how resources are distributed and used. Investigate the more hidden forms of authority that you have given or that your subordinates have taken. Discreetly interview those in your unit to find out how they see the resources being used. However, the outcome of this inquiry may yield multiple interpretations by different co-workers within the same work unit. One way to merge these different views is to observe how they actually complete their assigned functions while effectively employing the available resources. (Chapter 10 describes more fully how to integrate multiple perspectives.)

The next step is to begin negotiating the value of resources with those in your department and to encourage them to do likewise. When you and the members of your work unit trade resources with others, you can assess more readily the relative value of your resources. The value depends not just on what you can do with them but also on your relative need for them. The value of a resource's stock fluctuates according to the circumstances. For example, in the case of Chico, Chico's time increased in value when he took on a new department. Find the current value of your resources by negotiating with others.

The efficient functioning of your work unit depends on your being able to make maximum use of the resources you use. Don't let your resources lie fallow, unused and untraded in exchange for other, more valuable resources. Providing more resources than are needed—"excess capacity"—leads to inefficiency and waste. An efficient organization provides only the resources that are needed, sometimes even fewer than are needed.

Assuming that you've made optimum use of all your existing resources, you may still find that your work unit has to get by with less than adequate resources. If so, try to generate additional resources however you can. One way is for you to expand the resources at your disposal. This assumes that additional potential energy and talent are already present in the work unit, and that you can find ways to draw it out and use it. FTL offers a way to do this.

Invest in Present and Future Careers

One source of additional energy is the existing or potential expertise and motivations of the people in your work unit. By selectively investing your department's resources, you can gain a net increase in the resources within your department. Some of those investments will offer an immediate, if modest, return. Other investments offer long-term prospects for a substantial return on your investment.

The three primary forms of immediate, short-term, and long-term investment are task assignment, training, and leveraged investment, respectively. The most immediate way of getting a return on your investment is by carefully matching the *assignment of tasks* to the people in your unit who can accomplish them. A more substantial investment, which offers less immediate, but still short-term return on the investment is to *train* your employees to improve their effectiveness on their present jobs. The most significant—and the riskiest—investment is the *leveraged investment*, in which you invest resources in subordinates, on the assumption that they will outgrow their present jobs and assume more of your responsibilities so that you can outgrow yours.

Task Assignment

The people in your work unit probably have at least some skills and knowledge that are underemployed, talents that are underdeveloped, and work motivations and career aspirations that are at least partially untapped. A complementary source of additional energy is the motivational properties of the work itself. The trick is to match the skills and knowledge required by the work, as well as the skills and knowledge that can be gained by doing the work, with the relevant expertise, abilities, interests, and needs of your team members.

Conventional management strategies assign tasks to specifically titled *positions*, according to the official procedures, by following the written job descriptions explicitly. If the correctly titled worker is unavailable, the task usually must wait until such a person is available. If it is urgently needed, someone at a higher rank is given the task, as it is assumed that all managers can aptly perform all of the jobs of each of their subordinates.

Managers using FTL, on the other hand, tailor their task assignments to particular *people*, according to their uniquely individual abilities, motivations, and opportunities. FTL leaders also develop several alternative task-assignment plans. Each of the alternative plans is tried until one or a combination of them works well. While alternative plans are being explored, the unit's performance and output is monitored, and they maintain orderly relationships within the unit and in collaboration with other units.

For example, Ruth's and Tambuzi's groups in Chico's division developed alternative task-assignment plans within each unit, in order to capitalize on the available talents and motivations. They made plans to (a) lend specialists between projects as needed, (b) cross-train a few people, (c) send people outside for special training, and (d) groom backups for each task assignment. They understood that each plan must balance the unit's work performance with the need to maintain proper coordination with the other units.

Planning for the selective matching of specific tasks to specific workers requires a modest investment on the part of the supervisor. The return on the investment, however, is almost immediate. If the match was appropriate, the task will be accomplished admirably. If not, adjustments can quickly be made, and a more suitable match can be selected. A less immediate consequence of appropriate matches between tasks and workers occurs when a task is assigned that stretches the abilities of the workers, prompting them to increase their expertise or broaden their range of skills and knowledge.

Though all organizations specify task assignment in their written guidelines and customary procedures for employees, not all of them tailor the breadth of task assignments to match each task to a specific employee. For FTL managers, this growth process continues throughout the career of the employee. For conventional managers,

---

Exercise.

On several sheets of paper (one for each subordinate or co-worker whom you'd like to develop), make three columns. At the top of the page, write the name of the person. Label the three columns, "Skills," "Knowledge," and "Expertise to Develop."

In the skills column, list the things the person can do well that are "how-to" kinds of abilities (e.g., interpersonal communication in a small-group setting, manipulating tiny objects neatly and accurately). In the knowledge column, list the things the person knows "about" (e.g., the person's education and factual knowledge).

In the column for expertise to develop, list those areas of expertise that you'd like to have that person develop. These should be those things that are closely tied to existing expertise in order to allow the person to build on what is already known or mastered. Try to include those areas that you think the person would be most likely to be interested in.

Once you've done this for all the people in your work unit, go over your lists to make sure that the expertise you need developed appears on several places across the lists. Next, think about the kinds of resources you have available (or that you could trade with others to obtain) that would be needed in order to help this person to develop this expertise.

This done, you're ready to start your individual negotiation sessions with each person in the work unit, in order to offer opportunities for investment in exchange for development of expertise. This process is not identical to investment in order to encourage subordinates to grow out of their present jobs and to grow into yours, though it is very similar. And this process will provide you and your subordinates with experience in negotiation, to prepare for the more substantial negotiation for fast-track investment.

this process is only used during a narrowly prescribed period of time when training is expected to take place.

Training

Using FTL, a supervisor adjusts the difficulty and complexity of the task to the trainee's ability. Too difficult a task leads to frustration and failure; too easy a task can even be insulting. Ideally, this relationship develops into one of advisor and apprentice. Initially, the supervisor (advisor) explains the task fully to the trainee (apprentice), encouraging the apprentice to actively listen (see Chapter 2 for more on active listening) to the instructions. The advisor also makes clear what resources are available for completing the task and what authority is being granted to accompany the task.

Once a task has been assigned and the apprentice has acknowledged acceptance and understanding of the task, the apprentice owns full responsibility for that task's successful completion. The apprentice does not go to the advisor to have the advisor solve the problems, only for general guidance on strategies for solving the problem. When the apprentice is at a dead end, the advisor gives suggestions for alternative paths but does not recommend a particular path. Each time the apprentice reaches another dead end, the advisor suggests new alternatives, continuing to show patience and faith that the apprentice can solve the problem competently, given adequate guidance.

In contrast, many conventional managers follow the customary procedures and train their subordinates to follow (to the letter) all the official organizational practices. Further, conventional management procedures don't consider it necessary to communicate the rationale behind the procedures in order to have them implemented correctly. This can be a quick and inexpensive way to get people going on a job, but it generally works well only with simple, repetitive, and structured tasks (e.g., assembly-line operations). It does not work well for complex, nonrepetitive, and unstructured tasks (e.g., management).

Therefore, one quick way to identify whether people have developed under conventional management or under FTL is to ask them why they are doing a particular task a certain way. If they reply that they were told to do it that way, they were probably trained under conventional management procedures.

On the other hand, if they explain the rationale behind doing the task, they probably learned from an FTL leader. Only when people understand the rationale behind particular procedures are they able to monitor or judge their own performance. If they aren't able to evaluate their own performance, they can't determine how to improve or even how to avoid failure.

For example, three critical dimensions of productivity are speed, accuracy, and effective use of resources. For every task, different priorities must be assigned to each of these dimensions. For cutting diamonds, speed is far less important than accuracy and effective use of the materials. For microsurgery in the living heart, however, speed and accuracy may be more important than conserving the number of sponges and towels used. Moreover, if the diamond-cutter and the surgeon were to use the same degree of care and precision in a job moonlighting as salad chefs at Tostada Delight, they wouldn't last long on the job.

Apprentices who learn from an FTL supervisor find it easier and more rewarding to learn, due to a number of factors: (1) The lessons learned are relevant and personal. (2) Appropriate resources for learning are made available. (3) The learning process shows the apprentice how to understand and deal with the complexities in the organization. (4) Apprentices learn at their own pace and in their own directions. (5) Apprentices are encouraged to build on their strengths and to compensate for their weaknesses in other areas; they can therefore grow in a number of ways.

When apprentices are given the tools (resources, expertise, knowledge, skills) and the opportunities, they are able to develop their own competence in the tasks they undertake. By providing these tools and opportunities, the advisor communicates to the apprentices that they are trustworthy, competent professionals who are capable of managing their own careers, given adequate resources. "Instead of giving [the apprentice] a fish to eat, [the advisor] teaches [the apprentice] how to fish." This requires the apprentice to invest in the training process, as well as the advisor.

Investment

To tap human potential, you must invest in people. FTL helps you tap the human potential within your work unit. Unless you invest in the present and the future careers of some of the people in your work unit, their full potential will not be realized over the long term. I call this kind of investment "leveraged investment" because a large part of the investment you make is based on the credit (confidence in your competence and your trustworthiness) you have built with your subordinates. This investment is a long-term proposition.

You make a relatively modest investment of your present resources (attention, inside information about the organization, influence within the organization, latitude in performance of the job, access to departmental resources, critical assignments, and support) in your subordinates. In exchange, they make substantial investments of their time, energy, and personal resources in trying to outgrow their present jobs. But that's not where it ends.

Here's where the *leveraged* of *leveraged investment* comes into play. Your subordinates would not likely continue to invest this heavily if you hadn't also invested in them with credit you earned from your subordinates. The credit you have stems from your subordinates' belief that if they demonstrate that they have outgrown their present jobs, they grow into a more responsible job, initially at an informal level. At some point, they expect to be officially promoted and to be given a more prestigious job title and a higher salary than they have at present. If you aren't able to outgrow your job title, you'll be expected to create some intermediary job titles (with commensurate increases in salary and prestige) that go beyond the subordinate's present job titles. Ultimately, both you and they expect to derive payoffs reflecting a mutually supportive career-long relationship.

Thus, subordinates in whom you make a leveraged investment have taken a long-term view of career compensation. They recognize that they are not being adequately compensated for their extraordinary contributions at this time. However, they assume that in the future, they will be extraordinarily compensated for having done so. Remember that you have a long-term obligation to make such investments pay off for your subordinates. It's not unusual for an FTL retiree to continue to support previous apprentices, 30 years or more after their working relationship began.

Therefore, another quick way to identify types of development is to ask people whether they are compensated fairly according to their contributions to the organization. If they say they are treated unfairly because they are not paid enough or that they are treated fairly because they are paid in full for their contributions, they are conventionally trained. But if they say their treatment is fair even though they are contributing more than they are compensated for, they have probably been developed by FTL.

This is especially true if they go on to explain that they take a career-long perspective on the issue of compensation. From this perspective, young fast-trackers expect to be *under*compensated during the first half of their careers and *over*compensated during the second half. Therefore, when such young people are growing rapidly, they don't expect their immediate compensation to keep pace.

Rewards and Punishments

Conventional managers reward and punish people according to the official rules of the organization. Under this system, objective events are needed to justify official actions. The subtle aspects of performance therefore give way to actions that are publicly defensible (e.g., seniority takes precedence over merit). Such legalistic processes reinforce the bureaucratic tendency to "play it safe." Official rewards and punishments, when inappropriately applied, can demean, frustrate, and confuse employees.

Instead of hiding behind the immediate cash-and-carry exchanges of compliant behaviors for rewards and transgressions for punishments, FTL goes beyond them. It assumes that the true power of a management system lies in the building of a mature working relationship in which equivalent and leveraged exchanges are offered in terms of a long-term perspective. The supervisor offers added reinforcement of the day-to-day exchanges through inducements (investments in people) for contributions (performance).

Further, an even more subtle distinction must be made: Conventional managers believe that *they* must motivate their workers to perform; FTL managers know that only the individual worker can provide her or his own motivation. The leader can encourage and support the worker's intrinsic motivation—or even discourage it. But no one can put motivation into a worker who doesn't have it. Thus, each individual is assumed to be responsible for managing her or his own career.

Through FTL, you implement task assignment plans by negotiating various social exchanges with your subordinates: your inducements for your subordinates' contributions. You may offer your subordinates a challenging special assignment in exchange for investments in their careers. Several outcomes might result from these offers:

- A subordinate may politely decline the invitation, citing the lack of time to do the job right. This is a legitimate response if the special assignment is outside the subordinate's written job description (which it usually is).

  If it is the first refusal, you may make a few additional offers in the future.

  If the subordinate continues to decline such invitations, you may cease asking that subordinate.

  If the subordinate gets better without your help . . .

- If the subordinate accepts the invitation, one of two outcomes may result:

  If the subordinate successfully accomplishes the job, you'll continue with your plan to invest in that subordinate.

  If the subordinate fails in the next job, . . .

  If the subordinate doesn't successfully complete the job, one or more outcomes may result:

  You proceed with an alternate plan

  You may try investing more resources in aiding this subordinate   to complete the job more satisfactorily

  You may . . .

This is how a plan gradually takes shape. Both you and your subordinate make offers and accept or decline offers. Though you can't predict how the process will *unfold*, this is how it *works*.

Naturally, the assignments you offer are determined by the goals of your organization and the specific objectives of your work unit.

Goals and Objectives

The Conventional Approach

According to conventional management approaches, unit objectives are developed within the guidelines of the organization's official strategic plan, and programs are implemented to achieve these objectives. Higher-level management sets the overall goals, you set the objectives for your work unit, and your subordinates achieve the objectives you set.

You monitor the program's progress to keep them on time and on budget. You usually seek efficiency by cutting down on the time and the budget needed. The criteria for evaluating the program are set at the beginning and tend to be maintained throughout, sometimes even if dramatic changes occur in the program's relevance to the organization. You use oversimplified goals to chart organizational effectiveness. Annual goals are set to guide behavior and to serve as standards for evaluating effectiveness. Planners set goals, and workers are told to achieve them.

The FTL Strategy

Under FTL, managers are uncomfortable with such top-down goals. I call them "no brainers" because they are based on incomplete understanding of the constituencies that must be managed. Although some goals must be achieved to survive, such as profit, cash flow, and the like, other goals may become more or less important over time. It makes little sense to be very profitable one year and go out of business the next. Long-term survival requires that more goals be considered and that the relevancy of goals be evaluated more frequently.

In turbulent markets, survival requires flexibility both in the goals and in the means to achieve the goals. FTL supervisors understand that survival is affected by groups (constituencies) that have different priorities, and that these priorities may change over time. In fact, a program can be a success for one group and a failure for another.

Under FTL, supervisors enact strategic management processes with the people whom they supervise. People collaborate during all phases of the process, from problem-finding, through problem-solving and solution-implementation, to solution-evaluation. Supervisors sometimes enact feedback systems with their subordinates. These systems are tailored to the particular program and participants. Progress reporting may be immediate (if there are critical difficulties) or deferred until project completion (for smooth-running programs). Efficiency is achieved by discovering better methods of operating and for achieving high quality, not by squeezing time and budget parameters. This drive to become more efficient must guide the strategies you use *before* crises arise. During crises, you may not have time to do more than quick fixes that aren't carefully thought out and planned. Don't allow yourself to use the retrogressive attitude, "If it ain't broke, don't fix it." Or you could end up with a *lot* of fixing to do.

Networking Activities

The written rules and conventional procedures restrict the activity among different units through formal control devices. People are told how to behave, and steps are taken to prevent people from getting too involved outside of the unit. Under FTL, networking is encouraged. In fact, supervisors expand their influence by building networks outside their units through their own networking, and through the network contacts of their people. (See Chapter 6 for more on how to build networks.)

Summary

This chapter looked at the tasks of a work unit from two viewpoints: The conventional perspective, which seeks control through prescribed rules and procedures, and the FTL perspective, which allows flexibility to adjust to changes by developing long-term relationships with others and negotiating with them for the mutual benefit of all parties. FTL was shown as a way to turn the prospect of change from a disaster into an opportunity. Creative use of the conventional and the FTL perspectives offers insight into organizational effectiveness. Several additional reasons for using FTL were offered: (1) stress management and stress reduction for yourself and for your subordinates, (2) improved morale for your subordinates—and thereby for yourself, (3) response to extraordinary tasks, (4) response to changing circumstances, and (5) outdistancing your competition.

Four key features of FTL are growth, investment, focus, and integration. What you need in order to implement FTL are attractive resources, latitude in task assignment, motivated subordinates, support from your superiors, and your own self-motivation and competence. Several methods for capitalizing on FTL include (a) negotiating responsibilities, authorities, and resources; (b) investing in people through task assignments, training, and leveraged investments; (c) rewards and punishments; and (d) setting and reaching objectives.

The next chapter describes how to apply FTL in the wider contexts of the organization and of the world beyond it.

10

Discover the Whole Picture

Integrating Multiple Perspectives to See the Whole Picture

In Chapter 2, you were advised to focus in on your own work unit. Only when other work units directly affected your work were you to widen your focus. However, once you have analyzed your job situation, your career possibilities, and the internal functioning of your work unit within your organization, you're ready to think about how to succeed and perform effectively in your present job and how to outgrow it. To truly succeed and perform effectively, you must next broaden your view to see the whole picture of your organization. The *whole picture of your organization* includes all the various relationships among individuals, among work units, across departments, and up and down the organizational hierarchy. These relationships are intricately complex and must be understood in terms of both the officially documented realities (the written rules and the conventional procedures) and the hidden realities (the unwritten rules and the hidden strategies). The objective of this chapter is to show how to test the assumptions of the single perspective of officially documented reality or of your work unit, in order to integrate multiple perspectives into a whole picture of your organization.

Why is it essential to see the whole picture? Determining how to show that you are effective as a manager isn't easy. The superiors, peers, subordinates, other managers, clients, and suppliers who work with you every day seldom agree completely about your effectiveness. What's more, the very things that one of them considers a strength might be considered a weakness by another of them. (For example, what's a bargain for your client is a smaller profit margin for your supervisor.) Though they all make judgments of your effectiveness, they each use different *criteria* for those judgments. The differences in their criteria are based on their different objectives and goals for you. Even the ones who hold the same objectives may rank you differently, based on different priorities among conflicting objectives.

How can you possibly be perceived as effective in the eyes of all these different people within your organization, who evaluate your effectiveness from different perspectives? Naturally, it's impossible for you to please everyone all of the time in everything you do. Therefore, it's easy to feel that these conflicting views make it impossible to succeed within the organization. This sense of being overwhelmed by conflicting demands could lead to professional burnout and apathy. In order to avoid burnout, you must develop strategies for integrating their multiple perspectives. Using fast-track leadership (FTL), you can learn to manage success despite these opposing criteria for evaluating your effectiveness.

A Minefield of Multiple Perspectives

Carmen São Pedro, an accounting manager, is evaluated formally by Chun Yee, her supervisor, and informally by Pat, her peer, and Fran, her subordinate. Each of the three evaluators have different objectives for Carmen; each can affect Carmen, rewarding or punishing her to some degree. How should Carmen manage this minefield of conflicting expectations? If she continues to emphasize production, she pleases Chun, her superior, and she displeases her subordinate; accentuating Fran's career development causes the reverse. If Carmen chooses to focus on cooperation with peers, she pleases Pat and does not please either Chun or Fran.

Complicating this situation, Fran had previously developed a trusted assistant relationship with Mary, Chun's supervisor (i.e., Carmen's supervisor's supervisor). Fran had served as Mary's assistant before joining Carmen's unit. Carmen knows that Fran has talked to Mary about Fran's lack of support from Carmen. In fact, Fran had told Mary that she was seriously considering leaving the organization because of the lack of leadership in developing Fran's career.

Mary told Carmen that she had promised Fran that this situation would improve. Simultaneously, Chun has been pressuring Carmen to improve the production of her unit. Moreover, Pat has been seeking more cooperation from Carmen by inviting her to task force meetings. All of this comes to a head when Carmen's existing work load is taking nearly all of her time and energy—she has no slack.

Carmen must now decide what to do. Carmen's decision depends on how she evaluates the relative influence of each constituency. In this example, if Carmen pleases one of the evaluators by choosing any single goal, she does not please the other two. Carmen's analysis of this situation must consider both the obvious conventions and the hidden realities. Chun has the formal authority to give Carmen a poor performance evaluation, which may damage her career. Fran, by virtue of her relationship with Mary, also could damage Carmen's career. Finally, Pat, because he controls vital resources for Carmen's unit, could help or hurt the productivity of Carmen's unit and indirectly affect her career. Clearly, none of the three can be ignored. The problem is how to manage all three without suffering burnout.

Managers face these situations all the time. It would be much easier to be a manager if the manager had only a single set of compatible goals. Unfortunately, multiple constituencies exist and can be ignored only at great risk. The trick is to develop a navigation strategy that deftly maneuvers through the explosive minefield of displeased constituencies.

Fortunately, in Carmen's situation, not all the constituencies' goals come due at the same time. She has some time with which she can manipulate the conflicting objectives. If she can modify the objectives of the unit over time, she can direct the evaluations of the various constituencies. This may become a complex management task, but the benefits and the avoidance of injuries have important consequences for both her unit and her career.

Before deciding how to solve her problem, Carmen decided to investigate the situation further. She made it her business to discover each constituent's present situation. For example, she sought answers to the following questions, among others:

- What pressures was Chun getting from his constituencies, especially from Mary, his supervisor?
- Given that Mary was pressuring Carmen for greater development of Fran, was she also pressuring Chun on this issue?
- If this pressure from Mary was present, could it help Carmen to get some slack from Chun?
- Turning to Fran, what specifically did she want from Carmen?
- What actions would turn Fran around and please both Mary and Chun?
- Regarding Pat's requests, how could Chun be made to understand the benefits of improved cooperation between Carmen and Pat?

Carmen also uncovered hidden answers to her questions while seeking to formulate her problem. She used her network of trusted colleagues to help her get answers to some questions that she couldn't ask directly of some of her constituents. Once she had gathered this information, she could fully understand the problem: how to give each of her constituents what each really wanted.

Armed with this understanding, she formulated a solution that could spread her work into the future and could sidestep impending disaster. She would buy time by negotiating acceptable plans with Chun, Fran, and Pat now that she knew what they really wanted. Although Carmen never negotiated with Mary, the key to this negotiation was Mary (the supervisor of Chun, who was Carmen's supervisor). Unless Carmen's plans had a good chance of pleasing Mary, Chun would not allow Carmen the leeway to implement the three different plans.

Therefore, the target was Mary. Carmen never lost sight of her interest in Mary during her negotiations with Chun, with Fran (Carmen's subordinate), and with Pat (Carmen's peer). First, she negotiated a six-month program of productivity improvement with Chun, her supervisor. Then, with Fran, she worked out a career investment program based on annual assessments. Finally, she negotiated with Pat to develop a proposal for interdepartmental cooperation with reasonable target dates.

In her negotiations with Chun, she argued that all three plans would make him look good in Mary's eyes. Thus, it was in his best interests to support her plan. With Fran, she reasoned that Mary would be delighted with the opportunities designed into her development plan and would expect Fran to capitalize on them. Finally, with Pat, she emphasized that both Mary and Chun would be more receptive to a well-thought-out interdepartmental proposal from Carmen and Pat if Carmen had first gained Mary and Chun's support due to implementing the other two plans.

Carmen successfully maneuvered through this minefield of conflicting expectations by negotiating with her constituencies and spreading her obligations out over time. Before her negotiations, however, Carmen had taken the time to understand the hidden features of various constituencies, to project their actual assessment points, and to plan for these assessments. Once it was negotiated, while implementing the plan, she continually adjusted the plan to avoid getting off course.

Using FTL to Integrate Multiple Perspectives

In many real-life management situations, you are concerned with pleasing multiple constituencies: owners, management, customers, regulators, competitors, suppliers, employees, unions, the press, and various action groups. Each of these groups has the power to help or harm your unit; their divergent interests therefore must be integrated. Unless you can negotiate with constituencies and convince them to give you some latitude in meeting their demands, the only alternative to accepting the displeasure of some is attempting to satisfy all at the same time. The result is burnout.

You can request several forms of latitude from your constituencies: (1) modify their demands, (2) spread their demands out over time, (3) alter their criteria for satisfying those demands, or (4) create an alternative method for meeting their demands. In order to negotiate for an appropriate form of latitude to resolve conflicting and overloading demands, you must first understand hidden features of the whole picture of your organization.

Use this FTL strategy to create more realistic, more adaptable, and

more effective organizations. Many conventional management strategies are as effective in adapting to change as dinosaurs were in
adapting to the Ice Age. Incorporate the hidden strategies to help
your organization hold onto its competitive position in a changing
world. Look for both the obvious and the subtle features of the
whole picture of your organization.

Four Phases of Strategic Management

I call the FTL method that Carmen used "strategic management."
Strategic management allows a single individual to see the whole
picture beyond the conflicting narrow perspectives. By using strategic management, you can discover—and use effectively—the hidden features within the whole picture of your organization. To learn
about the whole picture on your job, you need the guidance of
people who have already mastered the hidden strategies.

Interdepartmental Apprenticeship Projects

The best way to learn strategic management is by using it on interdepartmental projects, with the guidance of someone who already
knows it well. Seek out ways to work on interdepartmental task
forces, perhaps by expressing your interest to your supervisor or to
your trusted colleagues. If possible, work with a superior on a strategic management issue in which you can take personal responsibility for the entire process, from *understanding* the issue (finding
and asking the appropriate questions), through *projecting* possible
consequences of plans (investigating the answers to the questions)
and through *planning* appropriate actions (making the proper recommendations), to *implementing* the action program (carrying it out).
   Throughout the process, you'll be *adjusting* each step to fit the
changing needs and situations. The phases of this process are shown
in Figure 10.1. (Adjusting occurs throughout all the phases.) It is
not unusual to return to an earlier phase because of questions raised
in a later phase. Like problem solving, strategic management is a
recursive process (each phase may be repeated one or more times
until you're satisfied with the outcome; recursive processes are described more fully in the summary for Chapter 7). In fact, the plan

Figure 10.1 *Phases of Strategic Management Process*

Understanding Phase

- Internal events of interest
  - —Strengths
  - —Weaknesses
- External events of interest
  - —Opportunities
  - —Threats

Projecting Phase

- Identify possible situational influences
- Estimate their probability of occurrence

Planning Phase

- Projections translated into action programs
- Feasibility studies
- Adoption

Implementing

- Action programs put in place
- Refinements

for strategic management has many features that resemble and overlap with the problem-solving strategy described in Chapter 7.

In a task force assignment, you work as an apprentice to the senior manager (i.e., a learner–advisor relationship more than a trainer–trainee one). As the apprentice, you seek only general guidance from your advisor when you have a problem. The advisor guides you and supports you but does not take over your project. The project is entirely your responsibility.

Your career objective in working with a task force on a strategic management issue is to gain an opportunity to outgrow your specialty and to use strategic management to grow into wider responsibilities. Meanwhile, for your specific project's objective, you'll develop one or more specific issues into implemented action programs.

To accomplish your career objectives, as well as your task objectives, the project must be meaningful, challenging, comprehensive, and timely. It must involve one or more important issues for the organization, must challenge you without defeating you, must involve several specialties, and must require the use of other staff experts. Finally, the project should involve issues that currently interest top management. In fact, the results of such a project should become part of the organization's own strategic management plan.

Understanding

During the understanding phase, your task is to identify and understand the various constituencies with vested interests in the project. The constituencies may include internal ones (e.g., stockholders, management groups, networks of subordinates) and external ones (clients, regulators, suppliers, competitors, unions, the press, various action groups, etc.). You should understand the interests of each of the constituencies, their priorities, and the impact they have on the project and the project's value.

You must also try to understand both the internal organizational events and the external environmental events. *Internal events* include such things as corporate subcultures, hidden agendas, intraorganizational competition and cooperation, conventional practices of the organization, and actions by any of the internal constituencies. *External events* include such things as market trends, political events, and actions by any of the external constituencies.

Finally, you need to study the side effects of the organizational initiatives that might affect other parts of the organization or its environment. That is, though only some of the constituencies may be involved in the pursuit of a solution to their problem, the solution they choose may affect other constituencies both inside and outside the organization. These are sometimes overlooked because the issues have been defined too narrowly. The study of possible side effects moves into the area of the next phase: projecting.

Projecting

In the projecting phase, you try to identify the events that might affect the organization and the probability that these events might occur. An obvious major problem of this phase is how to obtain accurate estimates based on logic rather than on hope or pessimism. One way to get accurate projections is to base projections on alternative futures: best case, worst case, and expected case.

Managers are usually surprised at how accurately this three-part method works. Using these three possibilities, educated projections can be developed and maintained, though they tend to become rapidly obsolete unless continually updated. During the projecting phase, questions may occur regarding your understanding of the project. These need to be answered before proceeding.

Planning

During the planning phase, the goals and objectives are translated into comprehensive action programs, specifying times for implementing each action. The key to the planning phase is choosing actions that can be effectively implemented. Thus, the action programs chosen must have a high probability of being implemented.

As with most other kinds of plans, the managers of the work units involved in implementing the action programs must also be fully involved in the planning. Unless people feel that they are involved in the planning, they hesitate to implement the recommended programs, or they implement them half-heartedly. This is not surprising. In order to feel committed to a project, you must be convinced of its merits. And in order to feel convinced of the merits of a project, you must also be involved in the understanding, projecting, and planning processes.

All too often, recent MBA graduates find that their new accounting programs, risk-management programs, or flexible manufacturing systems, which worked perfectly in the computer simulation, flop on the shop floor. One reason may be that people often resist a young manager's elegant new program. However, the young manager may be tempted to use resistance to change as an overall excuse for the failure of the program. Nonetheless, if the program doesn't work, it generally wasn't ready for implementation. In all likelihood, all the relevant people were not consulted in the action planning phase.

The planning phase proceeds from the general directions of the plan to the specific paths to take. Thus, you start with strategic issues, then move to long-term goals, then to short-term objectives and to action programs. Next, you consider the procedures for reporting the plan's progress. The side effects of the various action programs should be incorporated into the programs where appropriate. Finally, you develop contingency plans as much as possible.

When grappling with the strategic issues, ask questions about even the most fundamental assumptions underlying the plan. What business do we want to be in? What type of organization do we want to be? What size do we want to be? What management philosophy do we want? What time range and time increments do we want to use? Answer all of these questions so that managers do not develop conflicting sets of basic assumptions.

Once the strategic issues are set, the long-term goals can be determined. These should take into consideration the understanding reached about (a) each of the constituencies, (b) internal strengths and weaknesses, (c) external opportunities and threats, (d) side effects, and (e) projections of best, worst, and expected scenarios. General goal statements describe future desirable states of the organization, based on specific time ranges: 3 years, 5 years, or more. From these broad goals, more specific (and generally shorter term) objectives can be determined.

Statements of goals and objectives can be counterproductive, however, when they are used blindly or they outlive their usefulness. Managers periodically raise questions about the relevance and desirability of goals and objectives. When new opportunities or threats develop, effective managers try to reassess the goals and objectives, modifying them as needed. The balance between staying the course and capitalizing on changing circumstances is difficult to maintain. Conventional managers tend to err on the side of striving for a goal or objective in spite of changes in opportunities and threats; worse still, they may even be insensitive to changes.

Once the objectives have been determined, develop the highly specific action plans. The process of planning for action begins with generating ideas. Anyone on the task force (or the people in the competence network of any task force) can propose an idea. However, the idea generation and evaluation process is more formalized during strategic management than in general problem solving.

In order for an idea to be considered by the group, a *concept champion* must develop it and formally propose it to you, the project leader. If you are persuaded by the proposal, it proceeds to the informal feasibility phase, in which the champion directs a justification study. If this study is persuasive, a formal feasibility study is undertaken by the full planning group. If that's favorable, the adoption process begins. Preliminary designs of the components are made, and the program is written up in detail.

Table 10.1 *The Process of Action Planning and Implementation*

Phase	Content
Action Planning	
I.	Concept initiation
II.	Informal feasibility
III.	Formal feasibility
IV.	Adoption process
Implementation	
V.	Development of site design
VI.	Final working plans
VII.	Installation process
VIII.	Testing
IX.	Shakedown trial operations
X.	Operation

The action plans should confront the realities of the organization and its environment. Conventional managers like to keep the action planning process abstract and vague, avoiding the major operating issues and problems. However, you'll ultimately design a better action plan if you tailor it to the major operating issues. Where possible, try to incorporate the implementation process into the action plans.

An example of an action planning and implementation process is shown in Table 10.1. The process proceeds from concept initiation through the operation phase. Action planning comprises the first four phases shown in the table.

Implementing

The last six phases in Table 10.1 form the implementation process. A design is developed for the particular site, final working plans are drawn up, and the program is installed for testing. After the program components are installed, the process is tested on a small scale under controlled conditions. If this is satisfactory, full-scale operations are performed within a limited context. This allows testing of the effectiveness program and correction of whatever problems emerge before widening its application. Finally, the program is turned over completely to those who will operate and administer it; they run it according to standards established in the earlier phases.

The implementation phase usually contains the most difficult tests for your patience and adaptability. Erroneous assumptions, faulty reasoning, and unrealistic expectations seem to appear out of nowhere. However, if you have incorporated the implementation information into the action planning process, you can minimize some of this difficulty during the implementation phase.

When designing action programs, young managers commonly make the mistake of failing to tailor the program and the implementation process to the particular application. If the program is designed in isolation from the persons who will implement it, it stands little chance for success. For example, only a narrow range of the information needed may have been specifically requested by the solitary manager.

Solitary planning invites disaster. New programs *must* be tailored to particular applications by involving the people who will be operating the new program at all stages. Those affected by a new program must also have an impact at all stages. Involvement of the system users is a key FTL secret for successfully implementing new technology.

Adjusting

At each stage, from understanding through projecting and planning to implementing, the process goes back and forth iteratively through the adjustment process. Questions often need to be checked by reverting back to an earlier stage. The process improves through this sequence of finding questions, generating answers, and testing the answers in the reality of the implementation stage.

The key to successful competition in the marketplace is adaptable management. Survival of organizations demands adaptable managers operating within systems that encourage them to think and act to the best of their ability.

Exercise. Career Implications of the Whole Picture

Now that you have been given an overview of how strategic planning works, apply the techniques of strategic planning to strategically managing your own career. Get out your career notebook (which you started keeping in Part I of this book). Make notes of your answers to some of the following questions, and *write down* any questions you need to consider a bit longer before answering. Refer back to your questions, as well as some of your answers, at frequent intervals during your career. You may find that your answers change drastically as you advance in your career. And many of your questions will change as well.

Understanding

Your first task is to define your career problem (problem-finding): What do you want from your work experience? The answer to this question depends on what you really want from your life. Do you want your work life to be integrated into and to complement other personal goals? Or is your work life merely a means to have the resources to accomplish other goals? Is each job you have going to be an end in itself? Or do you want to use each job as a means to overall long-term career goals?

Assuming that you want a career instead of a series of jobs, what are your career goals? Do you want to use your employment experience to develop your ability to make real contributions in organizations? Imagine yourself at your retirement party. Make a list of those things you'd like to reflect on having achieved during your career. Don't just think in terms of financial achievements or specific tasks or projects. Include also the kinds of life-long working relationships you'd like to have built. Think about what you'd like to remember having contributed to others during your career.

Don't be overly conservative in your initial statement of goals. You'll modify this statement as you progress in your career, adding some goals and deleting others. Use these goals as the driving force in your career; allow them to guide your career choices. They'll help you to look beyond your immediate job situation to your alternative next step.

Once you've established (for now) your career-long goals, consider many options for how you can optimally achieve your career goals over your career. That is, after you decide where you want to go, you must consider how you're going to get there.

In thinking about how you're going to get where you want to be, your personal strengths and weaknesses can help guide your choices. What do you do well, and what do you have trouble with? Make a list of each. Be honest but not too tough on yourself. Include on the list those things you know about (facts, ideas, areas of knowledge) and those things you know how to do (skills, talents, technical proficiency). (You may want to refer to the lists you made for developing the expertise of others in Chapter 9.)

Add to your list any interpersonal and intrapersonal characteristics that help or hinder you. For example, an *interpersonal* strength might be that you enjoy meeting new people, and you know how to make strangers feel comfortable right away. An *intrapersonal* strength might be that you're enthusiastic about learning new things, and you work hard to find out things you need to know.

Include as many details on this list as you can possibly think of. Refer back to this list periodically, adding anything else you happen to notice about yourself. Ask family, friends, and co-workers for additional ideas or things they've observed about you—be sure to ask them for strengths as well as weaknesses.

Once you're satisfied with the completeness of your list, circle those of your strengths that will help move you closer to your goals. Next, circle those of your weaknesses that might hinder you in reaching your goals. The circled weaknesses are areas in which you need either to improve or to find strengths you can use to compensate for these weaknesses. Naturally, you should use the strengths you used to help you reach your goals and to match your capabilities to various opportunities.

However, don't forget entirely about those strengths you didn't circle. Even the most remote of skills pay off on occasion. For example, when you're negotiating a promotion campaign with a health-products client, it just might be an advantage to be able to sing the jingle while gargling with their new mouthwash. Don't discount *any* of your strengths.

Once you've evaluated your strengths and weaknesses in terms of your career goals, investigate the wide world of possible opportunities for you to use the talents you choose to use. Make a separate section in your notebook for keeping track of possible opportunities as you become aware of them. For each alternative, make a note of the potential opportunities and the possible threats each might hold for your career objectives.

Evaluate the alternative positions you're considering in terms of their relative opportunities and threats for your career objectives. What will each invest in your career, and how will their opportunities and threats match your capabilities and motivations? If a position is a good match, both you and the organization offering the position should benefit from the merger.

Projecting

Before selecting any of the positions, think about both the positive and negative situations that might develop on the job. This book has shown you a number of such possibilities. What are the likelihoods of these events in each of the positions you're considering? These are the risks as you see them. To find out about some of the possible situations, do your homework. Talk to people who should know; read everything relevant that you can get your hands on. Add what you find to your notebook.

Planning

Carefully develop your options for what you might do, evaluate each option, and then select a course of action. Once you think you've come up with a good alternative, try out your logic on trusted associates whose judgment you respect. Share your notes with them, and ask them to play the devil's advocate by searching for flaws in your plan. Be prepared for the most likely problems by developing contingency plans. And most assuredly, be prepared to modify your plan based on new information.

Implementing

Once you select a position, putting your plan into action requires continuing attention. You need to adapt constantly to the changing demands of your job situation. As suggested in Parts I and II, begin immediately to uncover the hidden features of your job situation and your organization. Based on this information, you can refine your plans.

In your work situation, identify the potential competence networks, and work to earn their acceptance. Of course, you will make mistakes, but you should treat them as opportunities for learning how not to repeat them. Collaborate with your supervisor to develop a true teamwork relationship. But don't lose sight of your driving force. You must manage your own career and earn the help of others in meeting your own objectives for your career.

Adjusting

Studies have shown that people who get the highest promotability ratings do *not* always get the highest job performance ratings. Moreover, the former more often get promoted than the latter. Those who are ready for a promotion are those who can effectively grow into the next-higher position rapidly. Outstanding performance in a lower position may not qualify you for promotion to a higher one. Thus, when you have a choice between becoming the best person on your present job in the organization and beginning to grow into the next higher position, your career plan will direct your choice.

To uncover the hidden features of your organization, notice the difference between working hard and working smart. Become alert to what things count toward promotion, and maximize your effectiveness on these things. Continually review your strategic career plan in order to keep it flexible and to capitalize on hidden opportunities. Keep the whole picture of your own career constantly in view.

A Plea for Leadership in the Global Picture

Another key to seeing the whole picture of your organization is to remember always that your organization participates in an even larger picture. Your organization doesn't operate in isolation. International competitiveness must be the driving force of organizations today and tomorrow.

Our country has recently suffered from a mindless arrogance spawned by our economic miracle of the 1950s and 1960s, during which time we consistently created over one third of the world's wealth with less than 6 percent of the world's population. In the 1970s and the 1980s, however, we have had to pay heavy consequences for this smugness.

If we are to reassert our economic leadership, we must once again capitalize on our native talents. We must reaffirm our belief that our culturally diverse people are our greatest competitive advantage in the international arena. We must share the secrets of the inside information and invest in the talented co-workers, subordinates, and supervisors within our organizations.

One great secret of international competitiveness that was lost during our two decades of tremendous prosperity is that an organization's investment in careers is not done out of altruism, but because it improves the organization's competitive position in its markets. Our foreign competitors understand this secret and are using it to their competitive advantage.

The challenge to our organizations is clear—find your competitive advantages and capitalize on them—all of them, especially your people. Now is the time for true FTL at all levels, but especially at the executive level.

Summary

This chapter began by considering a common source of managerial burnout: Managers are placed in situations of overloading and conflicting demands by their constituencies. To comply completely with these demands at any single time is physically impossible. One way to cope with these demands is to learn to integrate the diverse perspectives of the organization. By learning to discover and deal with the hidden constituencies within their organizations, a manager can solve complex problems by gaining latitude in pleasing their diverse constituencies.

This chapter introduces the opportunities to develop strategic management, which allows you to learn creative strategic management from a senior person. Special opportunities must be developed for you to learn it on the job from someone who already has the skill. Through these opportunities, you apply the processes of understanding, projecting, planning, and implementing. You thereby learn to rely on strategic thinking—essential to any leader. As the world market expands, strategic thinking becomes necessary for the competitive survival of U.S. organizations.

Finally, you should apply strategic thinking to your own career. Those who plan for the whole picture as well as for the immediate situation have an advantage over those who focus only on a narrow perspective. You need to manage your career by discovering your personal hidden strategies and matching them to gratifying career opportunities.

11

Teach Fast-Track Leadership

A Test of Fast-Track Leadership

Why isn't fast-track leadership (FTL) described in the management literature? It's difficult to describe, and many managers believe it cannot be taught. However, not only can it be taught—it has been taught.

My associates and I implemented an educational program capitalizing on FTL in an accounting division of a large multiplant organization. With the approval of the central office, we persuaded the accounting technicians and their immediate supervisors to receive training in a management system. Once they had learned the system, they were to use the system they had learned for three months after the training.

We wanted to test the effectiveness of FTL, as opposed to conventional management systems, so we trained the supervisors of half the units in FTL and the supervisors of the other half in traditional management. The greater improvement observed in FTL units could therefore be attributed to the FTL training, not just attention received for participation in a training program.

Training in FTL included the following:

1. *Understanding*. Describe the transformation of the working relationship between supervisor and worker from one of super-

visor and supervised to one of collaboration, in which each
worked to promote the career of the other.

2. *Projecting.* Discuss how this transformation can be brought about
   in this particular setting and with these particular subordinates.

3. *Planning.* Develop a script for the supervisors to follow when
   they first offered this new relationship individually to each of
   their subordinates.

4. *Implementing.* Have supervisors role-play this script to practice
   the necessary skills.

5. *Elaborating and Adjusting.* Instruct supervisors in methods of
   elaborating the new relationships through careful investments
   in their subordinates' careers.

Understanding

The concept of a teamwork relationship in which both work to promote each other's career was seen as highly desirable by most supervisors, but many doubted that their subordinates would want
such a working relationship with them. They saw their subordinates
as being content to do their jobs and to seek their satisfactions
outside of their work. However, when the supervisors were asked
if they had ever talked to their subordinates about what they wanted
from their work, they admitted that the subject had never come up.

Though most supervisors admitted that they could use greater
resources profitably in their units, they had never thought about
investing in their subordinates as a way of accomplishing this. They
protested that the pressure for performance in their units was intense, and they never had time to talk to their subordinates about
such matters. Some supervisors suggested that it may be too personal to talk to their subordinates about what they wanted from
their work. On the other hand, supervisors readily expressed their
own aspirations for growth and advancement in the organization.

One of the first things we had to do was to convince them to stop
thinking about their subordinates as people who were subordinated
to them, and instead to think of them as potential leaders just waiting
to be encouraged to lead. (Throughout the remainder of this chapter,
we refer to these people as "potential leaders" instead of "subor-

dinates.") In FTL, there is no such thing as "insubordination"—just ineffective leadership in encouraging your potential leaders to reciprocate for your investment in their careers.

Projecting

First, we discussed how this transformation could be brought about in their units, focusing on how to uncover the hidden features of their organization and their department. Next, we explored ways in which relationships with the potential leaders in each work unit affected the work unit's functioning. The five questions about their working relationship were discussed (these questions are described more fully in Chapter 8):

1. What do supervisors need from their potential leaders in order to do their jobs effectively?
2. What do potential leaders need from their supervisors in order to do their jobs effectively?
3. What are each person's job responsibilities?
4. What are the priorities for what should be done, and what actually gets done?
5. How do things get done when new situations arise?

Supervisors talked about the five questions and how each question applied to their particular work situations. They discovered that there were a number of ways that they could invest in their potential leaders. They also discovered that their potential leaders could promote them in a number of ways, as well.

Each supervisor also mentioned a number of actions that they had already taken in past situations that could be considered investment actions. In fact, all of them had, at one time or another, employed all 10 of the top 10 investment actions. However, their use of these actions was not a carefully planned feature of an investment strategy. Through these discussions, they came to realize that they could make these investments more thoughtfully and less clumsily. Further, because each of these actions had been tried before, they felt more assured that they wouldn't experience negative consequences from them.

Planning

In working out a plan for each potential leader, the supervisors developed a script that they could use to guide their initial offer of this new, reciprocal-investment relationship. The script required that they put themselves in the role of their potential leaders and see the conversation from that perspective. They needed to understand that this was the first time that the supervisor had asked what the potential leaders wanted from their work.

The supervisors also needed to understand the harm that had been caused by their having taken some of these actions in the past in a haphazard manner. Some of the potential leaders had been confused by only partial investments, after which the supervisor had not followed through with a more extensive and rewarding longer-term plan. Thus, the supervisors had lost some of their own credit for engineering leveraged investments. These issues had to be anticipated and effectively addressed in the script.

The script that was developed called for the supervisor to schedule a private meeting with each potential leader in order to discuss career plans. This meeting was introduced as an opportunity for both parties to talk about their work and how it could contribute to their career plans. The supervisor asked the potential leaders to talk about their likes and dislikes about the work, including their working relationships with their supervisor and their co-workers. The potential leaders were asked what they wanted from their work and from their careers with the organization.

The supervisors were advised that while the potential leader was speaking, the supervisors would write down notes and periodically ask relevant questions, but would not interrupt the flow of conversation. After the potential leaders had finished, the supervisors would talk about what they liked and disliked about their work and what they wanted in their career. They would describe the teamwork relationship in which each invested in the career of the other. The supervisors would then specify how this could be brought about with this particular person. Finally, the supervisor offered a teamwork relationship to the potential leader. If the person accepted the offer, they talked about some things that each could do to begin building this teamwork relationship.

Implementing

Supervisors became comfortable with this script by role-playing the anticipated interview while using different instructions. Each supervisor played each role under a number of different conditions. They took the role of supervisor dealing with potential leaders who (a) wanted to outgrow their job, (b) did not want to outgrow their job, and (c) had never thought about it. They also tried playing the role of each of the three kinds of potential leaders.

After each role-playing episode, they discussed the interactions and decided on the most appropriate behavior. From this role-playing, they learned the importance of active listening. By trying the role of their potential leaders, they saw that they had previously acquired the habit of passively listening: They would half listen to the person and half think about their own immediate problems.

In contrast, active listening required that they work to concentrate more of their attention on the other person's communications (see Chapter 2 for more on active listening). To aid in doing this, the supervisor took notes in writing and worked to ask relevant questions in response to the potential leaders' statements. These questions would both demonstrate understanding and test for proper interpretation of what was said.

Elaborating and Adjusting

In the final stage of the training, supervisors were instructed in methods of elaborating the new relationships through careful investments in their potential leaders' careers. They were guided to analyze their present job situations and discover or create latitude for them through hidden strategies. They were shown how and where to search for (a) the resources to invest in their people and (b) the actions their potential leaders could take to promote the supervisors.

They discussed the process of building such two-person relationships from an initial offer into a mature, team relationship. Questions were asked concerning the mutual obligations of the parties and the respective payoffs of each party. Supervisors came to understand that this teamwork relationship exceeded the typical employment contract. Therefore, potential leaders could not be ordered to do these extra things and could legitimately refuse their offers without jeopardizing their jobs. Thus, before they could proceed with the building of a teamwork relationship, the potential leader must first voluntarily accept the offer. Once they accepted the offer, the team building could begin on both sides of the relationship.

Results

Overall Success

Supervisors who had been trained in the practice of conventional supervision and had practiced it for an average of five years successfully learned and implemented this new leadership in their units. When we compared their units with those in which the supervisors were instructed in traditional management, we found gratifying improvements. The FTL-trained managers demonstrated improvements over traditional-management-trained managers in every area investigated, and we found no negative side effects.

The productivity of the FTL managers improved significantly over that of those using traditional management. In fact, the projected annual productivity savings were over 5 million dollars system-wide. Equally important, FTL units showed significant improvements in work motivation, leadership, and job satisfaction, compared to the traditionally managed work units.

In addition to assessing these performance measures after the new system had been in effect for three months, we examined more immediate results of our training four weeks after the end of training. We asked each of the potential leaders about their career planning sessions with their supervisors. Those in units where supervisors received the FTL training told us about exchanging information on what they liked and disliked about their jobs, about the relevance of their present jobs to their careers, and about receiving an offer of teamwork from their supervisor. In other words, the supervisors discussed what they had planned to discuss.

Clearly, our training was effective in terms of both the supervisors' behavior in the sessions and the gratifying performance results with their potential leaders. Only supervisors were trained in this study.

Their potential leaders were not. The potential leaders' understanding of this new system came directly from their supervisor.

Hidden Achievers

An equally important result of this investigation was that the potential leaders who reacted most positively to this new system were those who were underchallenged by the existing management system. In fact, these potential leaders accounted for almost the entire advantage in improvement: They improved their productivity over 50 percent more than the units operating under the existing system. This was accompanied by a vast improvement in their commitment to high productivity. Under FTL, previously underchallenged employees produced much more and liked it much better.

Imagine improving your personal productivity by more than half. This suggests that the existing management system tolerates or even encourages minimal performance. If FTL produced a 50 percent improvement in productivity, and the operators had no trouble maintaining it over three months, something's wrong with the existing system. Either it encourages this waste of human resources or it prevents the emergence of this potential.

In interviews with these newly high achievers after the experiment, they indicated that their work was now more relevant to their careers and that they now were getting somewhere in their careers. They found that collaborating with their supervisor in making their unit look good added personal meaning to their work. They did not want to return to the old way of doing things.

Replicating the Results

Another part of this investigation involved providing training to those supervisors who had not received it in the first round. That is, we offered FTL training to half of the supervisors who had served as the traditionally managed controls during the first part of the study. In this part of the study, we sought to prove that training would work for all of the supervisors, even those who were forced to wait for it.

Those supervisors trained in FTL six months after their cohorts were compared to the cohorts who received the traditional training, but no additional training. The FTL training was the same as that given six months before. Results of this study showed that the productivity of those units under the newly retrained supervisors improved significantly compared to that of the comparison units who had received no added training.

Equally important, the gain in productivity within the trained units was made by those who most wanted to outgrow their jobs. As in the first part of this study, those who most sought to outgrow their jobs were most likely to accept their supervisor's offer and to promote their supervisor by improving their productivity. Also in agreement with the first part, these previously underchallenged potential leaders produced an amazing improvement in productivity of more than 50 percent, and they had no problem maintaining it over a three-month period.

A Severe Test

This demonstration of the promise of FTL was remarkable because it was done in an organization that took pride in its enforcement of conventional procedures. Everything was to be done by the book —chapter and verse. Even though the central office had granted exceptional latitude for purposes of this study, upper management did not believe that either the supervisors or their potential leaders would adopt the new FTL procedures. Needless to say, they were astonished by the results. They had underestimated their employees—their potential leaders.

When these potential leaders were given both a way to outgrow their jobs and a good reason to do so, many chose to accept the invitation. From the organization's viewpoint, the results were extremely positive. Productivity was improved at very little cost. Potential leaders were outgrowing their jobs and enlarging the pool of promotable talent. Potential leaders were more positive about their work, their careers, and their commitment to the organization. Although management had underestimated its potential leaders, it had taken a risk and succeeded.

Nonetheless, that such hidden strategies can work so well even in organizations that pride themselves on enforcement of their conventional procedures should not be surprising. Most of what we call "leadership" resides outside of the conventional norms of management. Potential leaders often use exceptional methods for hidden reasons, in order to make the difference between success and failure in organizations. The hidden strategies need not be a violation of the written rules and conventional procedures. These may simply be used over and above what is specified by the written conventions.

In most situations, the mutual investment in each other's career by supervisors and their potential leaders does not specifically violate standard procedures. Instead, it goes above and beyond the customary expectations. Even in these organizations, those managers who can use these hidden strategies to tap into human potential create a competitive advantage for themselves and for the potential leaders in whom they invest. We attribute this advantage to FTL.

Show and Tell

The supervisors and managers in your organization would benefit from understanding the ideas of the FTL. Help them to learn. Too many managers assume that their potential leaders do not want to outgrow their prescribed jobs in terms of contribution and commitment to their organization. Comments heard by managers about "subordinates": "They only want to comply with the written requirements by employing the losing strategy of minimum personal cost"—which results in minimum personal gain. "Their favorite reason for not doing something that needs to be done and that they easily could do is that it's not my job—it's not in my job description."

On the contrary, we find that organizations contain many people who want to outgrow their jobs, as well as people who do not. Applying traditional management practices to those who seek to outgrow their jobs makes them frustrated and ineffective. Clearly, a different theory and practice must be employed for the fast-trackers to optimize their satisfaction and contribution to their organizations.

The Hidden Competitive Advantage

FTL is based on the assumption that organizations cannot survive in competitive markets without capitalizing more fully on the capabilities of their people. Following the hidden directives of inside information helps to optimize people's potential for leadership. Using these strategies, competent leaders can build collaborative networks and can make the difference between effectiveness and ineffectiveness in their organizations—or between thriving and failing in an ever-changing business environment.

I have described the processes by which people form effective teams within their work units, collaborative competence networks across departments, and collegial links with external entities. These links form a hidden infrastructure within the organization, which supports the operation of the organization and makes it more adaptable and competitive. Because the hidden strategies make organizations more adaptive as competitors, I have described techniques for discovering more about the inside of your organization and for employing this understanding to improve your chances of becoming a fast-tracker and building collaborative competence networks.

The key to all of this is gathering influence through relating to and interacting with *people*—and then using that influence to get things done. Potential influence awaits you inside your organization. I have described ways of finding, gathering, and using that influence for the good of your organization and your career.

See the Whole Picture

Finally, I suggested that you acquire skills for understanding and strategically managing the whole picture of your organization and that you apply these skills to your career. This brings us full circle back to you. Use this information to manage your own career. Your career is intimately tied to your constituencies: your supervisors, your co-workers, your potential leaders, and your colleagues. You can manage these relationships properly only from the inside of your organization. How well you manage these relationships will determine to a large extent how high you soar in your organization.

All the Best

My challenge has been to persuade you that you can improve your career effectiveness by dedicating your own driving force to riding on the fast track in your organization. I have shared what I have learned about the mysteries of this process and sincerely hope that you, the learner, will surpass by far the accumulated understanding of your professor. Pass it on!

For further information contact:

George Graen
7412 Towerview
Cincinnati, OH 45255

Index